Of Skies
and Seas

Library of Congress Cataloging in Publication Data

De Jonge, Joanne E., 1943–
   Of skies and seas.

   (My father's world)
   Summary: Twenty-three essays describe unique and
interesting facts about birds and sea creatures and remind us of
God's care for his creation.

   1. Birds—Addresses, essays, lectures—Juvenile literature.
2. Marine fauna—Addresses, essays, lectures—Juvenile
literature. [1. Birds—Addresses, essays, lectures. 2. Marine
animals—Addresses, essays, lectures] I. Bishop, Richard, ill.
II. Title. III. Series.
QL676.2.D4   1985   591   85-7391
ISBN 0-930265-11-4

Of Skies and Seas

Joanne E. De Jonge

Illustrations by Rich Bishop

CONTENTS

OF SKIES AND SEAS

You should have a kink in your neck when you're finished reading this book. Or at least you should be able to imagine a kink. This book looks up, far up. Then it looks down, far down.

You'll begin by looking up, at wonder pictures of the moon and stars and our galaxy and galaxies beyond us. Then you'll plant your feet solidly on earth, but still look up at the birds which glide overhead. You'll watch an eagle soaring above a river and feisty finches bickering about food. And you'll meet the rat patrol working silently in the dark of night. You'll take a break to meet Ollie, who can't fly, and turkies who don't care much about flying. But the geese flying south over your head will turn your attention upward one more time.

Then you'll look down, at dark silent places in the sea. You'll see rivers within oceans and valleys buried beneath six miles of black, near-freezing water. You'll meet the salmon that navigates those waters with ease, and the gentle manatee, whom navigating sailors believed to be a mermaid. You'll watch a hermit crab change its shell and discover a live "plastic bag." You'll meet my friend the lobster and you'll watch a flounder's eye migrate through its head.

After you've looked up and down, there will be no need to look around for answers to some common questions: Who threw the stars into the sky and guides those rivers within the seas? Who told the geese to fly in that perfect V and made the simple sponge so complicated? Who can explain that one-man show in blue and knows the recipe for a jellyfish? You'll know that the answer is written above and below you. You'll see that, in these creatures of skies and seas, *his* hand the wonders wrought.

1

Wonder Pictures

I have a very special set of photographs at home. They were taken through a huge telescope in Flagstaff, Arizona, and were given to us by Mr. Guetter, an astronomer who works there. I like to call them my "wonder pictures." I think you'll understand when I tell you more about them.

There are two special times when I take our "wonder pictures" out of the drawer and look at them. When I feel especially proud of something I've done, and I know I shouldn't be proud but I can't help it, I know it's time to look at the "wonder pictures." When I'm depressed because I have a problem that I can't seem to solve or I have to do something that I just don't think I can do, I get out the "wonder pictures."

The first picture is of the moon rising behind Mt. Elden, near Flagstaff. Along the bottom of the picture you can see the jagged outline of the pine trees on the mountain. Directly behind them, brought up close by the telescope, is a huge, light, eerie moon. You can see craters pockmarking its surface, and strange, huge, dark spots near the top. It looks so close you'd think you could walk beyond those trees and hop onto it, or at least reach out and touch it, but I know that's just a trick of the picture.

The moon is so far away, that, if it were possible to reach it by a car traveling as fast as we do on our superhighways, it would take at least 180 days of constant riding to get to it.

Even from that great distance the moon affects our earth. The force of its gravity pulls at the water in our oceans and creates the tides. Some scientists even say that the moon's gravity pulls at our dry land and raises it almost four and a half inches certain times of the day.

The temperatures of the moon are so extreme, we would almost boil in the light and certainly freeze solid in the darkness. Just walking from the light to a shadow, we would feel a difference of 200 degrees Fahrenheit in temperature.

I suppose I see the moon just about every night, but I don't really think about it—how far away it is, how it affects us, and even how it stays there, reliably circling the earth—until I look at that picture.

The second picture is of the constellation

Pleiades, or the Seven Sisters. There are four very bright stars, several smaller stars bright enough to make little X's in the picture, and hundreds of little white dots.

If you find this constellation in the sky, you can easily see six stars; with sharp eyes you can maybe count nine. The telescope shows us that within this "little" group of stars there are really hundreds of stars that we can't ordinarily see. That one picture has more stars than I would care to count, and that's only one little piece of the sky.

When I try to think about how far away the stars in the Pleiades are, I can't imagine it. It took the light from those stars four hundred years to reach the earth. The light that we see left those stars long before Columbus reached America. This means that those stars are 2,400,000,000,000,000,000 miles away from us!

The stars in the Pleiades are part of our galaxy, the Milky Way Galaxy. There are many, many more stars in our galaxy, maybe as many as 200 billion. They're spread across such a great distance that it would take light 100,000 years to travel across the whole galaxy.

I wonder if any person can really imagine just how many stars there are in our galaxy, and just how far away all those stars are!

The Milk Way Galaxy isn't the only galaxy whirling around in space. The third picture is of another whole galaxy, the Whirlpool Galaxy. Just like the Milky Way, maybe even bigger, it contains

billions and billions of stars. The distances between these billions of stars—which look like a little white blotch on my picture—are measured in trillions and trillions of miles, more miles than we can count.

This Whirlpool Galaxy looks close to us in the picture, yet it's many times farther than those stars in the Pleiades. It took the light from these stars in the Whirlpool Galaxy 3.7 million years to reach the earth. The light that the telescope recorded when it took that picture left those stars long before we think the history of people began.

I wonder if any person can possibly imagine the billions of stars there are in that galaxy as well as in ours, and I wonder if anyone can really understand how far away from us the Whirlpool Galaxy is.

The fourth picture looks like little pinpoint stars against a black night. Mr. Guetter told us that they aren't stars; they're galaxies. In this one picture alone there are about 500 galaxies. Each of these galaxies has about 2 to 20 billion stars in it—stars like our sun, some bigger, some smaller. Imagine, 2 to 20 billion suns in each galaxy, and 500 galaxies in this picture of one patch of sky!

I wonder just how many galaxies there are, and how many stars in those galaxies, and how many trillions upon trillions of miles away they are.

My mind is too small to even try to understand

the numbers of galaxies and the distances involved. So I mentally put myself back through trillions of miles to our own Milky Way Galaxy. I think of that one rather ordinary star that we circle—our sun—and I think of the moon that circles us, still so many miles away, and I wonder.

I wonder how I could ever be proud of myself, one little person on one little planet circling one little star. How puny I must seem in the eyes of such a great God who can count all those stars and galaxies and who can measure all that distance, and who made them all and keeps them all in their courses.

I wonder how I could ever feel depressed over a problem that I thought I couldn't solve. This God who created and counts stars and the galaxies has promised to be with me personally and to help me with all my little decisions and problems. How wonderful!

My "wonder pictures" are very special to me because they remind me of my God, so great that he made the universe and so good that he even takes an interest in me.

You can have your own "wonder pictures" too. All you have to do is go outside on a clear night and look up at the stars.

2

The Way of an Eagle

"There are three things that are too amazing for me, four that I do not understand: the way of an eagle in the sky. . . ." Prov. 30:18–19a

High above the Muskegon River an eagle surveys his domain. Soaring on warm air currents, he barely moves a muscle as he scans the river and surrounding land below him. Suddenly he folds his enormous wings and dives to tree-top level. Swiftly he opens them and resumes his silent patrol. No noise betrays his presence, so graceful and silent is he. Only a shadow, moving like a swift, silent cloud, alerts a woman standing in the woods below.

She knows he is a bald eagle; she has briefly glimpsed his brown body and snow-white head and tail. But he is gone as quickly as he came; he circles once and leaves. She knows she cannot follow him.

Quickly he regains altitude and soars directly above the river. Searching the water, he spots a fish near the surface. Once more he folds his wings and plunges. His powerful feet strike the fish beneath the water. Cold water splashes his wings and his breast, but his body stays above the surface. With a few strong wingbeats he rises, the fish in his talons.

Silently he carries it to a gravel bar where he begins to feed. Holding the fish with his powerful feet, he tears off bits of flesh with his strong, curved beak. When he is finished, he lifts his enormous wings once more. Gradually he glides to his favorite perch, a branch high on an old dead pine, and surveys the river once more.

This eagle has lived by the Muskegon River with his mate for several years. Few people live nearby, and fewer still know of the eagles' nest. Those that know care enough to let these magnificent birds live in peace.

His mate, perched nearby, is slightly larger than he. Her wings measure almost seven and one-half feet from tip to tip; his measure seven feet. Both wingspans are longer than a full-grown man is tall. These enormous wings, combined with strong breast muscles and broad tails, allow the eagles to make pinpoint landings as they hunt.

Silently the female searches the far riverbank.

Her eyes, like those of her mate, are big, bright, golden yellow, and very sharp. She can spot a tiny creature far below, a white rabbit sitting on snow a mile away, or large game almost three miles distant.

Her eyes are surrounded by a ring of bony plates. This protects them against air pressure when she dives at speeds close to 175 miles an hour. She has three eyelids—an upper, a lower, and a side lid. This third, transparent lid she pulls over her eyes as she dives, to keep out dust.

Now she drops off her perch, opens her wings, and makes a sharp turn. She has spotted a mouse. She cruises along the river at speeds up to forty miles an hour for a few seconds. Then she swoops, or dives, rises again, and flies to the nest. The mouse dangles in her talons.

Like her mate, she has four long, sharp talons, or claws, on each foot. Three are pointed forward and the fourth, a full two inches long, is turned back. They are curved so that she can grip her prey. They're joined to her toes in such a way that she can move them easily.

Bumps on the middle joints of their toes afford the eagles an even firmer grasp on their food. The lower parts of their legs are scaled rather than feathered. Scales dry faster than feathers and are easier to keep clean.

She picks at the mouse with her strong hooked beak. There are two nostril holes in that beak, but they are protected inside so food and dust can't slip in and suffocate her. Although it is

strong, her beak is also light. An eagle must have no extra weight as it flies.

She has finished her meal and turns her attention to her mate. She has been with him since she first mated—ten years ago, when she was four years old. She could be with him for many years yet. Eagles mate for life and live to be twenty or thirty years old. If one of them should die, the other would take a new mate.

But they are still together and it's early spring, the mating season. They spent the winter ranging far from the nest. By night they had rested on a few favorite perches. By day they had hunted scarce rodents and fish. Now they have returned to the nest they have used each year. Soon they must repair it. Now they will court.

Suddenly the male drops from his perch and soars skyward. The female follows. High above the river they soar in large circles. The male climbs high above the female, closes his wings, and plummets toward her like a thunderbolt. She turns on her back, talons up, greeting her mate in midair. They lock claws and, fastened together, tumble and roll through the air, separating only when they near the ground. Opening their wings, they scream and swoop upward on warm air currents.

For many days the eagles swoop and dive, tumble and play together. They are not silent because they are not hunting. They are enjoying the free, natural life of bald eagles.

Far below them on the riverbank a woman

watches in silent wonder. Their screams have told her that the eagles will soon be nesting. She knows what will happen next, although the birds will be far from prying eyes. She's content now to watch as they soar and tumble high in the sky.

Both in form and in action, the eagles are magnificent birds, bearing witness to a Creator who is ever so much more magnificent.

"Does the eagle soar at your command and build his nest on high?"

"Everything under heaven belongs to me."

—Job 39:27; 41:11b

3

The Eagle and Its Young

. . . like an eagle that stirs up its nest and hovers over its young, that spreads its wings to catch them and carries them on its pinions.

—Deut. 32:11

High above the Muskegon River the eagle pair has been courting. Mates for life, they still court early every spring. Rolling and tumbling through the air, screaming and swooping, they have alerted the woman who stands on the river-bank. She knows that soon they will be nesting.

Their nest, however, is far from prying eyes. Already they have begun to repair it and add to it. Six feet high—about as tall as a man—and just as wide, the big nest is almost flat. The female has already added some soft leaves, grass, and feathers to the slight hollow where she will lay her eggs. Around these, branches and twigs are woven to make an untidy-looking cradle.

The eagles have taken only a week to repair their nest. Young eagles building a new nest may take two to six weeks to complete their work. This eagle pair, like most eagles, returns to the same nest yearly and adds to it. Sometimes a nest may grow to be almost ten feet across and twenty feet deep.

The female lays an egg in the nest; two days later she lays a second egg. Immediately she settles herself over them. The eggs must be kept warm at all times. If they were left alone, the cold, early spring winds would freeze them. But they are kept warm under her soft belly feathers.

The female, or eagless, looks at her mate perched nearby. She is hungry. Immediately he swoops from his perch and soars over the river. Minutes later he returns with a plump duck in his talons. Carefully he holds it on his perch with one foot and plucks out the feathers with his beak, working for thirty minutes until the duck is clean. Then he flies to the nest and carefully places it by his mate.

When the eagless has finished eating, she chirps to her mate, who flies to the nest. The eagless carefully picks up the duck bones and flies away while the male settles over the eggs.

For thirty-five days the eagles take turns incubating the eggs. Usually the eagless stays with the nest while the male, or cock, hunts for their food. If intruders come or animals threaten, the cock chases them away. From time to time the eagless rises, bends over, and gently turns the eggs with her beak. Other times she rises to fly, and the cock settles on the eggs.

Finally the eagles hear a soft chirping inside an egg. Chirping back, they encourage the little eaglet to break the shell. It's a long, hard struggle that takes many hours. Finally, using his egg tooth—a knob at the end of his beak—a male eaglet wiggles out of the egg. He's exhausted.

Often a female eaglet is bigger and stronger than a male when she hatches. She can easily take away his food, push him from the nest, or peck him to death. That's why a male eaglet usually hatches first. He has about two days to grow before a female hatches. Then the male is big enough to defend himself.

Now both eggs have hatched. The eagless has carefully removed the pieces of shell from the nest and settled gently over her young. When the weather is chilly, the downy chicks must be kept warm. They must also be protected from the hot sun and the rain.

Once more the male eagle swoops from his perch. He must hunt often now because he has a family to feed. Silently he returns with a mouse in his talons. He drops it in front of the eagless, who rips it apart and feeds it to the chicks. Should any of the chicks eat fur, bones, or feathers which they cannot digest, they will cough them up as castings. The eagless quietly picks these up and throws them from the nest.

May has now warmed into June, then melted into July. Both adult eagles have fed their young. They have given the eaglets bigger and bigger chunks of food. As the little beaks grow and talons become sharp, the eaglets have learned how to tear their own meat.

Both eagles have defended the nesting territory against other hunting birds. If too many birds like them were to share the region, their food supply would run short. Also, the little eaglets must be protected from birds that might harm them.

Now it is early August. The eaglets are almost three feet tall and have brownish feathers. They will exchange their brown head and tail feathers for white ones in four or five years, when they are ready to mate. Now they are ready to fly.

Once more the male eagle leaves the nest and returns with a fish. This time he ignores the hungry chirpings of the eaglets and eats the fish himself. Soon the eagless follows her mate's example. She refuses to feed the young. For two days they ignore the eaglets' cries. It's time for the young to leave the nest.

Early on the third day the cock catches another fish and flies close to the nest, dangling it from his talons. Excited by the food, the male eaglet hops to the side of the nest, reaches out, and falls. But he doesn't fall far. Soon he's flapping his wings and flying for the first time. The other eaglet soon follows him.

Both birds have much to learn. They're awkward in flight. Their wing and tail feathers are a little longer than adult feathers. This gives them a little extra lift for the first few weeks of flying. They're also clumsy hunters. They must try again and again to snatch a fish from the river. So they will stay with their parents, learning to hunt from more experienced birds. They will still eat at the nest when they have caught nothing for themselves.

On the second day of flight the young male makes a grave mistake. Soaring high above the river, he spots a fish. Folding his wings and plunging, he doesn't stop soon enough. He crashes into the cold water. The strong current sweeps him downriver as he rolls over and over. Finally he's swept to a gravel bar, where he comes ashore gasping for air. Weak and tired, he flaps his soggy wings as he awkwardly bumbles toward shore. Now the exhausted young eagle has pulled himself onto dry land and flopped down on his belly. His parents circle and cry overhead.

For hours the helpless, tired young eagle rests in the sun. One of his parents is always nearby guarding him. Occasionally they will bring him a fresh fish. They do not leave him until he is dry, strong, and ready to fly again. Then they will be ready to teach him.

Now it is late August. Both young eagles have learned much about flying and hunting. They may stay with their parents all winter, or they may leave. Today they are hunting with their parents.

High above the Muskegon River, four eagles survey their domain. No noise betrays their presence, so silent and graceful are they. Only large shadows moving like swift, silent clouds alert a woman standing in the woods below. She knows the eagles have raised their young successfully. She knows how much care they have given their young. These magnificent birds are such watchful parents, bearing witness to a Father ever much more watchful.

He satisfies my desires with good things so that my youth is renewed like the eagle's.

—Ps. 103:5

4

Those Feisty Finches

The first time I saw goldfinches I figured that they were probably the most feisty birds around.

We had hung a finch feeder on our balcony. The feeder itself was rather delicate, as feeders go. The perches were only an inch or two long. No grackle or blue jay could fit even one toe on a perch like that. Those perches definitely were made for delicate little finch feet.

The holes where the seeds come out were so small, they were hardly visible. A cardinal certainly couldn't pick a seed through such a tiny hole. Those holes were definitely made for delicate little finch beaks.

Even the seeds were tiny. Thistle seed, we were told, is finch food. Each seed is not much bigger than a comma on this page—delicate little seeds for delicate little birds.

Our delicate little feeder hung for about a week before it was noticed. Every day I'd peek, hoping to glimpse a tiny yellow body flittering about. I always peered around the edge of the window, figuring that such little birds would probably scare at the slightest movement.

Then they came—twenty-six of them in one shot. I wasn't watching at the time, but I couldn't miss them because they set up such a ruckus. Chirping and peeping, they scrambled all over each other, trying to get at the feeder and at the extra seeds spilled on the balcony.

I walked right up to the window to count them, and they didn't mind a bit. In fact, they were so busy arguing among themselves they didn't even notice me.

That's when I figured that they were the most feisty birds around. *Feisty* means "cocky," "spunky," almost "quarrelsome," and that's exactly what those finches were. I promptly dubbed them our "feisty finches."

In a way, I was a little disappointed in our finches. I had expected such little birds to be shy and skittish. Didn't they know that they were tiny and should be scared? Besides that, there wasn't a bright yellow one in the lot. They were all a drab olive. Didn't they know they were supposed to be bright yellow? What was wrong with those feisty finches?

Of course, nothing was wrong with the

finches. I just didn't know much about them. I had seen them first in November. By then they had put on their warm winter coats with over a thousand extra feathers each. Both males and females wear drab olive colors in the winter. When spring comes, the birds molt. That's when the males put on their bright yellow feathers to impress the females. The females keep their drab olive color, which makes them less visible when they're sitting on their nests.

When spring came, the finches still weren't behaving quite as I expected them to. After the males put on their bright yellow coats, I expected each of them to claim a territory and a female, and then settle down to the business of raising a family. Lots of birds operate that way.

The male finches won females all right, but they didn't bother to claim territories. They also didn't seem very interested in family life.

Throughout May and June we watched phoebes, robins, and blue jays raise families. They all worked hard and usually silently to feed their young. But those feisty finches bickered at our feeder as if they had nothing better to do. Each finch couple's biggest worry, it seemed, was to dominate the feeder. They set up their usual ruckus whenever more than two were together.

By the time July rolled around, I had given up expecting anything except bickering from those feisty finches. Of course, I was surprised again.

Suddenly, as if on cue, they changed drastically. They didn't look different, but they acted differently. They still bickered at the feeder—I suppose they always will—but the males started flying differently. They'd zoom all over the yard, one after another, looping around as if they were on a roller coaster. They'd keep it up for twenty or thirty minutes without a stop—zooming and looping at top speed. You'd think such little birds would wear themselves out in a hurry, but they didn't. They zoomed and looped for days.

Of course, that was a signal. Those feisty finches were finally ready to settle down and raise a family or two. Finally, they were claiming territories. That's what all the zooming and looping was about.

Through the rest of the summer the finches calmed down just a little bit. At least the females did. Female goldfinches spend most of their time on the nest after they've laid eggs. The male will fly near the nest. If the female is hungry, she'll give a soft little call and the male will come and feed her. He'll also help feed the chicks when they hatch.

For a few weeks last summer we saw mostly males at our feeder. We figured that they were raising their families.

When they finally get down to business, goldfinches sometimes raise two broods within one summer. They may start late, but they're all business when they finally do get started.

September was well under way by the time the finches had successfully reared their second broods. In fact, I was a little worried about them.

The days were shorter and cooler; winter was coming on. Didn't those feisty finches know they should have started sooner if they wanted to raise *two* families?

I didn't have to worry, of course. Little finches stay in their nest about two weeks. By the time they leave, they're as feisty as the adults. They call loudly and fly swiftly. They follow their parents everywhere, even to our feeder.

Now it's autumn and the finches are molting again. Soon they'll all be dressed in their warm, drab, olive coats. They'll be ready for winter. Some of them will fly south, but many of them will stay right here.

I'm looking forward to watching the finches this winter. This year I know a little more about them. At least I've learned that in the bird world, small doesn't automatically mean shy. What the finches lack in size they make up for in spunk. I won't expect them to act the way *I* think they should act. My ideas are all wrong for them. I'll expect them to act the way they were created to act. That's right for them.

5

Rat Patrol

Satellite Beach, Florida, had problems with rats. The little—actually not-too-little—varmints were getting into garbage, running up and down telephone wires, and making a general nuisance of themselves. In desperation the city fathers called the Rat Patrol, which promptly took control of the situation and the rats.

A certain man once had a cellar full of rats. He bought a few cats to take care of the rats. Every evening he put the cats in the cellar. Every morning when he opened the cellar door the cats bolted out, hissing and spitting with fear. They must have been 'fraidy cats. Finally, the man called in one member of the Rat Patrol. In a few days the rats were gone.

This Rat Patrol sounds like a pretty efficient organization. Do you know any of its members? They're not TV stars who ride around the desert enforcing the law. They're not even a group of men who get rid of rats for a living. They don't ride up to your house in a van, and they don't answer if you call the local pest control service.

The Rat Patrol is a much more efficient organization than any of these. In fact, each member does a pretty good job single-handedly, because each member was especially created for its way of life. The Rat Patrol is simply all the members of the owl family.

There are at least three hundred different kinds of owls found all over the world. They live in forests, deserts, swamps, fields, mountains, and at seashores. You can find owls in the frigid Arctic and in the steaming tropics. Each type of owl looks, sounds, and lives just a little bit differently from every other type of owl. Each fits perfectly into its own environment.

Most owls are gray or brown with broken patterns of lighter and darker feathers. This makes them almost invisible against the bark and branches of trees in which they like to sit. The snowy owl, however, is white. It likes to feed along shorelines and in snow-covered north country. It can hardly be seen in light sand dunes or above white snow.

Most owls like to take up their patrol duties at night, so God gave them the right equipment to use at night. Their eyes are much sharper than ours, especially at night. We have cells called rods in our eyes to help us see in the dark. We also have cone cells to help us see color. Owls' eyes are packed with rod cells, many more than we have. A night that seems dark to us looks only like a hazy afternoon to owls. They don't have much room left in their eyes for cone cells, so their world is colored in various shades of gray. Color makes no difference to them. What matters is that they can see even a small glimmer in a rat's eyes.

Most birds have eyes placed on the sides of their heads. Owls' eyes are placed in the front of their faces. Vision from each eye overlaps and helps them judge distances between them and their food. That's important for a creature that hunts.

Because an owl's eyes are in the front of its face, the bird can't see much of what's going on behind it. It really doesn't have to when it's out cruising for rodents; they certainly won't be flying behind it. But just in case it wants to see far to the side or behind, it's been given a special neck.

Humans have only seven neck bones. That seems to be enough for us. Owls have fourteen neck bones, attached to some very strong muscles. An owl can turn its head almost halfway around without much trouble. I suppose it doesn't do that much when flying at night, though. The most it would see would be the moon.

Owls have very sensitive ears, a definite advantage during the darkest night. Most birds only have small ear holes, which open on the inner ear. Owls are the only birds that have small flaps of skin near the ear holes. These skin flaps help channel the sound into the inner ear. They work as our ears work, only better.

Owl ears are set far apart on the head. Sound waves from a rustling rat usually reach one ear just a split second before they reach the other ear. This helps the owl detect exactly where the sound is coming from.

The feathers that ring an owl's face are controlled by certain muscles. Some people think that owls adjust these feathers precisely to funnel sounds into their ears.

Most birds have firm, strong flight feathers on their wings; so do owls. But the edges of owls' flight feathers are soft as down. This makes their flight silent. A rat usually can't hear a member of the Rat Patrol sneak up on it.

Owls have four long dagger-like talons on each foot. The outer talons can be swung out for a better grip on the prey. When an owl grabs a rat or a rabbit it seldom lets go.

Owls have a strange way of eating. They usually gulp down their prey—bones, feathers, fur, shells, and all. Anything that can't be digested is churned into a tight oval bundle, and the owl gulps that back up and spits it out. These little bundles are called owl pellets.

In the interest of accuracy, I must admit that

not all owls are members of the Rat Patrol. Small owls seem to make fine pest controls. They eat grasshoppers, caterpillars, moths, beetles, spiders, frogs, salamanders, mice, lizards, and small birds.

Large owls, such as barn owls and screech owls, eat rats, field and wood mice, squirrels, gophers, skunks, rabbits, birds, and fish. Barn owls and long-eared owls eat little else besides rats, mice, and other harmful rodents. Two barn owls working together to feed themselves and their family may capture up to fifteen hundred rodents—mostly rats—in three months.

If you ever want to call in a member of the Rat Patrol, you may have trouble finding one. City fathers in Satellite Beach obtained their owls from a wildlife society. I don't know where the man with the 'fraidy cats got his owl.

Owls usually shun contacts with people. They prefer to stay quietly in or on a tree during the day. Because they fly so quietly at night, people are often not aware of their presence. The coos, whinnies, wails, hoots, and screeches that you may hear occasionally are usually uttered to a mate. An owl usually doesn't hoot while it's hunting. That would give away its presence, and owls don't like to do that, not even to people.

If you do happen to see an owl, consider yourself fortunate. And give it a salute; after all, it's a member of the original Rat Patrol.

6

Our Blue Jays

Besides filling our bird feeder last winter, we put out ears of corn. Wayne attached some boards to the corner of our balcony railing, pounded nails through the boards, and pushed a big ear of corn onto each nail. We settled down in our living room to watch the birds gratefully flock to our newly expanded "restaurant."

The bird feeder fared well, as usual. It served mostly sparrows and juncoes and demanded re-filling weekly.

The ears of corn were rejected, however. For at least three months the same two ears stood nailed to the board, untouched. We changed the ears once, reasoning that the first ears may have been "bad," or the wrong color (how can corn be the wrong color?), or the wrong shape (it looked like normal corn to me). Still, the birds spurned our corn.

We decided to outwait the birds. Either they would eat the corn, or the corn would stay there forever. They'd have to look at it every time they went to the feeder. Besides, leaving the corn out there was easier than taking it in. And we had a half-bushel stashed away in a corner of the living room, awaiting the run-on-DeJonge-corn that never happened.

Finally, in early spring, our stubbornness (or laziness) was rewarded. One morning, as the sun was rising and we were trying to rise, we heard a "blonk" against our balcony railing. The rail actually vibrated like a rubber band. It sounded like our balcony had fallen off the building. A big blue jay had landed.

Every morning for a few weeks after that we shared our coffee-quarter-hour with blue jays. We'd hear them screeching and calling in the trees first. Then one would pass in a flutter of blue wings. Finally a jay would land heavily— blonk—next to the corn, and begin to eat— bonk, bonk, bonk. Each time a jay pecked a kernel from the ear, the whole balcony vibrated. It sounded more like a noisy jackhammer than a bird.

We enjoyed our jays. They were noisy, but that helped us wake up. They were bold. We could open a door three feet from them and talk to them, and they'd talk back. They were big—ten to twelve

inches long. We could see them even through half-open eyes. They were beautiful. Their bright blue feathers, I thought, were gorgeous.

We assumed that our jays had come from some place south of us when the weather had warmed. We had had blue jays around all winter; they do weather some pretty tough winters. But, I'm told, the jays we have in the winter generally move farther north for the summer. Our summer blue jays have been "south" for the winter. Last winter we must have had no-corn-eating winter jays. In the spring we had corn-eating summer jays.

Some people raised an eyebrow or two when I told them we were feeding blue jays. After all, many people believe that jays are bold rascals. Keep blue jays at your feeder, they say, and the other birds will leave. Some people even told me that blue jays are bad. I simply shrugged, said that they must have been created for a purpose, and dropped the subject.

I almost argued about it once. The fellow in the local music store cornered me and ranted about the blue jays in his yard. Apparently some jays had raided other birds' nests and taken eggs. He said that they had also taken some newly hatched chicks. He for one, he said, was not going to let blue jays into his yard. (Right then I had visions of him flapping from treetop to treetop, patrolling his yard.) What good were blue jays? he challenged me. How does a bird like that have a place in creation?

I thought of arguing about the balance of nature; maybe there would have been too many birds that spring. I wanted to tell him that their "good" probably outweighed their "bad." I thought of saying, "It's one of God's creatures. It's here for a reason." But I had come in for violin strings. I have a one-track mind and can't think about blue jays and violin strings at the same time. So I grunted and left.

Anyway, our jays also stayed. By late spring and early summer we didn't see or hear them as much. I think they were nesting. Blue jays are very quiet and cautious when they're raising a family.

When the blue jays disappeared for a while, I looked beyond our balcony to what had been a field. Bulldozers and heavy equipment had rumbled in. A new street lined with seventeen duplexes took shape. Our field was gone.

Many of our birds were gone too. I think the more timid birds may have been scared away by the construction noise. Maybe some of their natural food was gone. Our field had become a suburb, and not all birds like suburbs.

One Sunday in late July I saw our jays. I was walking in the back yard when I heard a quiet commotion in the poplar trees. When I walked over to the trees the commotion became loud. The jays were scolding me for coming too close to them. I spotted two jays on a top branch making all the noise. Then I saw why they were nervous. Perched on branches near them were four young jays. They were probably out of the nest for one of the first times, and the parents were rightfully a little nervous about my presence.

By late summer our jays were as noisy and sassy as ever. Their family was raised and adapting well to life in the suburbs. They'd talk back to me again when I scolded them from the doorway. They'd squawk noisily when a neighbor's cat walked past. Nothing could scare those bold birds away.

Last week, as I put out another ear of corn, I thought about our blue jays. I'm really glad that God made such bold birds. After all, what would happen if all birds disappeared when people moved in? We'd have a lot more insects in our cities, certainly. What would we do about that?

Besides, wouldn't life be dull without those saucy blue jays? I don't know whom I'd watch or laugh at or scold every morning. Who else would eat our corn . . . and whom could that fellow in the music store complain about?

7

News from a Pheasant

A pheasant woke us up this morning with some good news. He didn't know it, I'm sure, but all his squawking and wing-flapping gave us several welcome bits of information.

He told us that it was morning and that the sun was up. He also told us that he had survived another night safely. Every night when the sun goes down, he announces to the world that he's going to his roost. We hear him squawking and flapping his wings for a while, and then he's silent. He prefers to roost in a marshy area because night prowlers like foxes, skunks, or cats can't reach him easily there. He usually flies a short distance before he lands in a tree. That way he leaves no trail for his keen-nosed predators.

All night he sleeps on a branch of some tree in the field; when the sun comes up, he comes down. He squawks and flaps and announces to the world that he's safe and it's time to start another day. Sometimes his day starts a little earlier than ours, but he doesn't hesitate to tell us that he thinks it's time to get up.

He told us that he's claiming most of the field as his territory. We first heard him arguing— with himself, I think—down by the stream. After a short silence he called from the west end of the field to anyone who would listen. A few minutes later we heard him strutting and "muttering" as he took up his station just below our window. Later we heard him near the road on the east side of the field. He squawks so loudly, you'd think he's really bothered about something. But the only thing bothering him is that he must claim his territory in the spring and defend it from other cock (male) pheasants. Each area in which he struts and calls is his "crowing area," marking the boundary of his territory. All his crowing is simply telling other cock pheasants that they are not welcome. His territory probably covers several acres; some cocks claim as much as twenty acres for themselves. He's gone through this routine for several mornings now and we haven't heard any arguments lately, so he must be getting pretty sure of his territory.

Soon he'll tell us that he's ready to mate. He'll call from each crowing area again but stay in each area a little longer. He'll use it to show himself off to any female pheasant (hen) that happens to wander past. We love to watch this display. The field isn't completely covered with new growth by this time, so we can usually spot him; and he always lets us, as well as the hens, know exactly where he is. Accompanying himself with a loud call, he'll strut in front of the hen, displaying his brilliant green head and long, multi-colored tail to his best advantage. The hen, a little smaller than the cock and colored in mottled browns, doesn't always seem interested. She's usually picking at young plants and seeds. All his showing off must have some effect, though; usually he wins not only one but two to five hens.

During the summer the pheasants tell us more by their silence than by their calls. If all is well with them, they won't make much noise. Only when they're bothered or when they go to roost do we hear them. The cock usually does nothing during the summer but enjoy life, eat, dust his feathers, and sleep. He did his work when he won the hens; now he lets the hens work to raise the chicks.

The hens are very busy. They make their nests in little hollows right on the ground, lining them with grass. The hens blend so perfectly with the underbrush that they usually can't be spotted when they're sitting on their nests. When their broods of ten to twelve chicks hatch, the hens take good care of them. They lead the chicks along "pheasant paths"—their own footpaths—

in the morning to look for seeds, berries, and insects. When the sun grows hot, they lead the chicks to dusting areas to cool themselves and idle away the day. If the night is cool, they'll nestle the chicks warmly under their feathers. If any predator finds them, the hens will hop off their nests and try to lure the danger away. The chicks will stay with the hens all summer, until they are fully grown.

Of course the hens are silent in the summer. They don't want us to know where their chicks are. We consider ourselves fortunate if we happen to spot them in the underbrush. Last summer we seldom saw them. Only once was I able to count two hens and eleven half-grown chicks.

But that was last summer; the pheasants have yet to mate this spring. The cock told us that loudly this morning.

He told us one other bit of welcome news; he is still there and using the field. Last spring five new houses were built on the edges of the field; two more were added this spring. There's less field this year and more people, dogs, and cats. During the winter we worried that the pheasants might move away, like the more timid birds and the deer did several years ago. But pheasants are bold birds and adapt themselves quite well, as long as some of the field is left.

When the pheasant woke us up this morning, he told us that the sun was up, he was claiming his territory, and he was going to stay for another year. And we were glad.

8

Dumb Turkeys?

Turkeys, turkeys, turkeys! We surely get enough of them around Thanksgiving. Cardboard turkeys—fat and healthy with their tails spread out to their fullest—decorate homes and classrooms alike. Grocery stores advertise bargains on turkey meat. Magazines offer advice on how to buy them, how to roast them, how to carve them, and what to do with the leftovers. And, of course, there's always at least one article telling us about how dumb turkeys are.

Last year our newspaper devoted a three-page article to the dumbness of turkeys. It told me, among other tidbits, that when flocks of turkeys on turkey farms are frightened they panic and crowd into a corner to hide, smothering themselves. It said that turkeys are about the dumbest of birds—able to escape through the tiniest hole in a fence but completely unable to find their way in again.

I had always ignored that turkey talk before, but with that article I had had enough.

First of all, it's always been hard for me to make the connection between a living, breathing, fully-feathered turkey (dumb or not) and that golden-roasted "bird" that appears on our Thanksgiving table. I hate to mentally follow the turkey through its last agonies.

Second, and much more important to me, I can't accept the idea of a dumb bird. Although I've been told again and again—even by turkey farmers—that turkeys are not at all intelligent, my mind keeps telling me that I've never seen a dumb piece of creation. I just don't think that God would create a dumb bird.

Last year I decided to investigate a bit to find out if turkeys really are dumb. This is what I came up with.

There are two very different types of turkeys in North America—wild and domesticated. Wild turkeys once flourished from Maine to South Dakota, and south to Mexico and Guatemala. They were hunted so extensively that they almost became extinct in some places. The last wild turkey disappeared from the New England states over one hundred years ago. In recent years, however, the number of wild turkeys has increased.

Wild turkeys are basically ground birds and feed on insects, fruits, and acorns. They're always ready to raid a nearby cornfield if possible. At night they roost in trees, preferably in inaccessible swamps to provide safety from their enemies. That certainly doesn't sound dumb to me!

They like to roam in small flocks. Often two turkeys in a group will become very attached to each other. If separated, they will do everything possible to get back together again. During mating season, the cocks (males) and hens (females) roam together. When the hens are ready to lay their eggs, they separate. The cocks move on and the hens stay with the nest.

Wild turkeys are the most fun to watch in April, their mating season. The cock is hopelessly vain. He struts in front of a hen with his feathers ruffled, his tail raised and spread, his head ornaments swelled, and his wing quills drooping and rattling. The hen, as if sensing that he could strut forever if she allowed him to, throws herself at his feet. Each cock may claim three to five hens as mates.

All this strutting about would be tiring for any turkey, but the male is especially equipped for it. Just before mating season a large amount of fat accumulates in his breast. This serves as a storehouse for energy, supplying the cock with plenty of calories for all of his showing off.

When the hen is ready to lay her eggs, she'll build a nest on the ground in a wooded area. She's very cautious, carefully approaching the nest from a different direction every time she comes to it. While she's brooding her eggs, she's silent—not uttering a call—so that no one, not even the cock, can find her.

Sometimes two or three hens will all lay their eggs in one nest and take turns brooding the eggs. That certainly doesn't sound dumb to me!

Turkey chicks often accumulate biting ticks in their downy fluff. To rid themselves of these ticks, they instinctively waddle to an abandoned ant nest and roll in it. Ticks can't tolerate the odor of ants, so they fall off immediately. Pretty clever, eh?

Wild turkeys have become very wary of people and will not readily show themselves. They are strong fliers and can run long distances without becoming fatigued. They will give any hunter a very tiring chase. That's downright smart, especially during turkey hunting season!

Although the number of wild turkeys is rising again, domestic (tame) turkeys have never been close to extinction. They're raised on turkey farms all over the country. Since Thanksgiving Day has become an annual event in the US and Canada, turkey farming has become a big business.

By controlling the mating of turkeys artificially, farmers have raised bigger, juicier, meatier (more white, less dark meat) turkeys. But the turkeys raised on turkey farms hardly resemble the wild turkeys from which they were bred. They're more tender, fatter, healthier—and dumber.

Domestic turkeys are the turkeys we eat over ninety-nine percent of the time. Domestic turkeys are also the ones people probably talk about (when they talk about turkeys) over ninety-nine percent of the time. When people say that turkeys are dumb, they mean domestic turkeys. That doesn't bother me at all.

When people were breeding turkeys for more and better meat, they probably bred the smartness right out of the bird. You can't eat intelligence, so no one worried about it. God didn't create the domestic turkey. It's just people's "handiwork" after trying to improve on the original model.

God created the wild turkeys intelligent enough to live in their own world and to occasionally even fool a hunter or two. Now I feel a lot better about the whole turkey business. We have plenty of domestic turkeys around, raised for eating and made "dumb" by man's meddling. The intelligence of wild turkeys isn't in doubt any more. Now I can eat the domestic bird, raised for that purpose, and admire the wild bird.

9

Big Red

Everybody likes Big Red. In fact, Big Red is such a well-known, popular bird that I'm not going to tell you exactly who he is. Not yet. Try to guess.

You realize, of course, that Big Red isn't an individual bird. He's a certain *kind* of bird. The Big Red who comes to my feeder isn't the same Big Red who comes to yours. But he looks the same.

One of the reasons for Big Red's popularity is that he's so pretty. His brilliant red coloring immediately attracts attention. Even his stout little beak is red. A bright red crest jaunts from his head and makes him look rather perky. Dabs of black around his eyes and beak give him even more character.

Do you know who Big Red is? Imagine a rather large red bird that you've seen. That's Big Red.

Red-Brown is Big Red's mate. Everybody likes her too, but probably not quite as much as they like Big Red. That's because they don't notice her as quickly.

Red-Brown has the same crest, the same reddish beak, and the same dabs of black as Big Red. But where Big Red sports a brilliant red, Red-Brown dresses a bit more soberly. She likes a little red, but a lot of brown mixed in with it.

She's got a reason for dressing this way. It is she who sits on the nest. Were she bright red, any enemies could spot her instantly. So she dresses to blend with the shrubbery that surrounds her nest. That's good protection for her young.

Another reason that everyone likes Big Red is that he sings so well. So does Red-Brown, although she sings a bit more softly. One of Big Red's calls sounds just like a little bell ringing. And he sings throughout the year. So if you have big Red around, you also have beautiful music in the area.

A third reason people like Big Red is that he seems to like people. Some birds are very shy of people, but not Big Red. Give him some open space—he doesn't care for forests—and a bit of dense shrubbery for Red-Brown's nest, and he's likely to move in. Houses and people don't bother him.

In fact, Big Red has been moving to new places. About one hundred years ago he was a rare sight in the United States, except in the South. He never wandered up as far as Canada. But as people cleared forests and made meadows Big Red moved in, even into cities. Now he's moved as far north as Nova Scotia and Ontario in Canada. He's also spread west into Texas, South Dakota, and Manitoba. Everybody's welcomed Big Red.

People also like Big Red because he often stays when he comes. Many Big Reds don't care to take Florida vacations during the winter. They'll stay right up north, thank you. They're a beautiful sight on a snowy landscape.

Everybody who knows Big Red also knows that he has a craving for sunflower seeds. Throw a few sunflower seeds out regularly and you're likely to have a pair of freeloaders on your hands. He also eats berries, corn, and a few other tasties, but sunflower seeds are his all-time favorite.

Now do you know who Big Red is? What bird do you know that goes bananas for sunflower seeds? That's Big Red.

If you've ever watched Big Red, you probably know this next part. He likes to come to your feeder, especially at dawn and dusk. He often comes by himself first and looks over the place. Then he gives a "tink tink" call; he sounds like a little bell. Soon Red-Brown joins him.

You may have even seen him feeding Red-Brown. He does that often in the month of March, before and while she's building a nest. That's his way of courting Red-Brown, telling her that he wants to be her mate. He cracks open a seed and offers her the meat inside. She takes it right from his beak. She's telling him that she'll be his mate.

Surely, now you know who Big Red is.

Red-Brown builds her nest just a few feet off the ground in dense shrubbery. She fashions a deep, open nest and lines it with soft material. Then she lays three or four bluish-white, brown-spotted eggs. She sits on those eggs for about twelve days, until they hatch.

For ten days after the chicks hatch, Big Red and Red-Brown have their hands—or wings—full. They must feed each yellow-brown chick almost one and one-half times its weight in food every day. Usually they feed insects to the young birds. Insects are a little easier to eat than hard seeds.

As soon as the chicks leave the nest, Red-Brown takes off. She must build another nest and start her second (or third) clutch of eggs. Big Red stays with his chicks a little longer. He teaches them how to find food. When they're able to take care of themselves, he leaves to help Red-Brown with the new family.

If you don't know who Big Red is by now, I'd like to tell you. But first review the facts for a final guess. Big Red is a brilliant red bird. His mate is reddish-brown. He sings well, likes people, and loves sunflower seeds. He often feeds his mate and checks the safety of a feeding area before he calls her. He helps feed the young, and he teaches them what every little cardinal should know. That's it—Big Red is a cardinal.

I think that cardinals are a special delight in creation, don't you?

10

Meet Ollie

Ollie is really a different bird. I'd avoid him if I were a bird. When someone—or some bird—is *that* different, you can never tell what he's going to do.

For example, many birds have pleasant songs. Some of them may screech a little, but they still sound like birds. But Ollie's voice has been described as a "grunt," and as a "boom-boom." What normal bird grunts or goes "boom-boom" when it tries to sing? Ollie does. I don't know if I would trust any bird that grunts when it should sing.

Most birds build some kind of nest, or at least use a hole in a tree or a cactus. Even birds that nest on the ground often scrape some sort of nest together. Not Ollie. I must admit that he scrapes a little hollow in the ground, but not much of one. It's a wonder any of his eggs survive. Ollie must be awfully lazy. He builds such a different nest. I don't know if I would trust a bird that makes such a strange nest.

Most birds lay a reasonable number of eggs, but Ollie's mates almost go wild. Ollie usually has three, sometimes six mates. (I don't know if I'd trust any bird that has over one mate at a time.) Each mate lays six to eight eggs. They lay all their eggs in the same "nest." Ollie has from ten to forty eggs in his nest. Sometimes he even has fifty eggs. And they're all mixed up because all the females laid them in the same nest. Besides that, Ollie usually stays on the eggs. One female might sit on them for a while, but only during the day, and only if the weather is cold. Usually Ollie can't even cover all those eggs with his body. Some of his eggs just don't hatch. I don't know about Ollie's bunch. They surely take care of their eggs differently from most birds. And so many eggs! Don't they know when to stop? I'd stay away from Ollie and his bunch if I were a respectable bird.

Most birds have three or four toes. Usually, they have some kind of claw at the end of each toe. Ollie has only two toes. They're not even matched well; one toe is much bigger than the other. He doesn't even have real claws on those two toes. He has a toenail type of claw instead, short and stubby. I'd stay away from Ollie. He's so different. You never know about two-toed birds.

Most birds are quite small and beautiful. A few birds may be big, but not Ollie. He's *huge*—too big for a self-respecting bird. He weighs between 300 and 350 pounds. That's almost as much as the weight of two men put together. Besides that, Ollie has a neck that's between two and three feet long. Perched on top is his tiny flat head with his flat bill and big eyes. He even has eyelids with eyelashes. Now what self-respecting bird has eyelashes? How can he even call himself a bird with that long neck? If I were a bird, I'd simply ignore Ollie. He doesn't deserve to be called a bird.

Now *this* takes the cake. Ollie can't even fly. He's too big and heavy, and his wings are too small. Ollie's just made all wrong for a bird. He gives birds a bad name. If I were a self-respecting bird, I'd either ignore Ollie or try to get rid of him. He's a disgrace to birds.

But God didn't ignore Ollie. In fact, he made Ollie just the way he is, and it's really perfect for Ollie's type of life. And we're not birds, so we don't have to become upset about Ollie spoiling our reputation. We can just look at him and enjoy him for what he is. You see, Ollie is an ostrich.

Maybe Ollie can't fly, but he can run as fast as forty miles per hour. He can outrun most of his enemies, so he doesn't have to worry about flying. Those short wings are just right for helping him keep his balance when he runs.

Maybe most self-respecting birds don't have eyelashes, but Ollie's surely come in handy. Ollie lives in a dry, dusty region of Africa. His eyelashes help keep the blowing dust out of his eyes.

Ollie's eyes are big; his whole eyeball is almost as big as a tennis ball. The part that looks out on the world is bigger than the whole body of a little bee hummingbird. Ollie's eyes are also sharp; he can see better than we can.

His neck may be long, but that puts his head with his sharp eyes about eight feet above the ground. Ollie can look above the heads of most animals.

Ollie's toes are really just right for him. Long claws would get in his way when he walks. Short toenails don't. I understand that those feet with only two toes each can be dangerous to Ollie's enemies. Because he has such long, strong legs, a swift kick from Ollie is like a swift kick from a horse. Ollie can gash or tear a lion or a jackal with one swift kick. Ollie's feet are just what he needs, although other birds might not understand.

Ollie's mates do lay lots of eggs. That's their way of instinctively making sure that some eggs will hatch each year. Because ostrich eggs are on the ground, hyenas and jackals often eat them. Because there are so many eggs, some always hatch.

Other birds may not understand Ollie's nest, but it's just right for him. Of course it's on the ground; Ollie can't fly. Ollie buries the eggs part way into the sand to protect them from rain. He makes a shallow trench around his nest to keep water off the eggs. When he sits on the nest, he usually stretches his long neck and his head along the ground. That way, animals don't easily see Ollie. Ollie really does take good care of his eggs.

Does Ollie's voice really grunt, or go "boom-boom"? That's what people say. It may not be a beautiful bird call, but it does attract mates for Ollie. I'm sure that he's satisfied with it.

Other birds, if they could think, might not understand Ollie. They might ignore him because he is different from most birds; he's almost strange. I'm sure that Ollie doesn't mind. After all, God didn't ignore him. God made him just right, although the other birds might not think so. I'm sure Ollie is glad that God doesn't ignore "different" birds. I know I'm glad that he doesn't ignore "different" people.

11

One-Man Show in Blue

By September (which is early spring for birds that live south of the equator), the satin bowerbird is well into his act. He usually starts in July and keeps it up through January. I'd love to watch him at it, but he lives clear over in Australia. I guess I'll have to settle for pictures and descriptions.

You may wonder what's so special about the satin bowerbird. After all, he's only a bird. Why should I be so interested in that particular one? I can watch plenty of birds right here.

It's his act that makes this bird so special. I'm told it's quite a show. You could call it a one-man show in blue.

Before I tell you about his show, let me explain part of his name.

The satin bowerbird is not made of satin, although he's called a *satin* bowerbird. He's made of feathers, like any other bird. But the feathers are so glossy they shine like satin. Hence the "satin" part of his name.

I say "his" on purpose (though the name really applies to both males and females). You see, the females and the young are a slightly speckled olive-green color. The satin shine shows on them, but not as well as it does on the adult male. He's a solid blue-black, so he really shines like satin.

The "bower" part of the name also comes from the male, and it refers to part of his act. He does it all for the female, but *he* does it, so I shall call this bird "he."

He begins by making a bower—a little shelter of twigs. He's really fussy about the twigs he selects, and he makes his bower just so. He builds it right on the ground, making two walls, each about a foot high, about five inches apart from each other. Then he "paints" the walls with a mixture of saliva and charcoal, berries, or dirt. The walls curve inward a little at the bottom and meet to form a floor. So he has a little walkway between the walls.

He almost always builds this bower in a north-south direction. The walls are on the east and west sides. So when he walks through it, he's facing either north or south.

After the walls and walkway are finished, he builds a "front porch," a little platform of twigs at the north entrance. This "front porch" is really important to him. That's what he uses for a stage during his show.

Next, he goes out and collects all the props he'll need for the show. This can be quite a show in itself. He picks up some natural things—feathers, snail shells, flowers—and places them carefully on his porch. But he also picks up manufactured items—pieces of crockery, drinking straws, little toys, marbles, anything that suits his fancy.

Somehow, the color blue really suits his fancy. His first choice is always blue objects. People have found blue clothespins, toothbrushes, pens, buttons, toys, lipstick cases, and all sorts of other things in his bower. Anything that's blue and small enough to be carried isn't safe if the satin bowerbird is preparing for his show.

In fact, anything blue isn't safe even on his platform. Other bowerbirds in the area just might come by and steal it for their own platforms. But then, he might steal it back. There's a real run on blue things when satin bowerbirds are sprucing up their acts.

Having only a few objects won't do. This bird seems to feel that he needs all the props he can get. He can collect up to three hundred props before he feels that he's ready to begin.

When he's ready to begin his show, he finds a female and somehow lures her into his bower. He always brings her in through the back door so that she's facing his stage. Then he goes into his act.

He steps out onto the stage and picks up one of his props with his beak. Then he hops in front of her, fans his tail, flashes his wings, and makes a funny sound. You can almost imagine him saying, "See this pretty blue clothespin? Isn't it an object of delight?"

He sets down one prop and picks up another. "Now this snail shell isn't blue, but it certainly is beautiful." Again he hops, fans, flashes, and makes a funny sound.

Down the second prop goes and up comes a third. "Now check out this beautiful blue marble. Let me hop a little closer so you can see it. Isn't it the most beautiful blue marble you've ever seen?" Hop, fan, flash, funny sound.

On and on he goes, showing off all his worldly goods to the female he wants to impress. The show can go on for thirty minutes without an intermission. The poor female just sits and watches the male show off. Finally, he wears himself out and the show stops.

Usually the birds mate in the bower, but they don't raise a family there.

The female builds a nest and cares for the young alone. While she's taking care of the family, the male stays at his bower. In fact, he repairs his bower, adds to his collection, and puts on his one-man show for other females. This goes on for months. It's a continuously running one-man show in blue.

He's a real ham, the satin bowerbird. He loves to show off and impress the ladies. His blue act is a real show-stopper. There's none other like it.

Why in the world do you think he goes to all this trouble? He certainly puts on an elaborate show. Of course, he does it to wow the ladies, but some birds wow the ladies by simply standing in front of them.

Maybe female satin bowerbirds *are* impressed and *do* enjoy the show. I know I would. I even like the pictures and descriptions. I think that I would find the show absolutely delightful.

I can't help thinking that God made some parts of his creation just for sheer delight.

12

Who Told the Geese?

Last night we heard geese fly overhead. We couldn't see them because the night was dark, but we could hear them honking at each other. As I lay in bed listening, I pictured those birds overhead. Flying in perfect V-shaped formation high above a darkened landscape, they were migrating south. Some had made the journey many times, but in the dark night they had no landmarks to guide them. Some were probably making their first flight, but they too knew exactly where to go. Some would travel for thousands of miles, but they would return next spring. And they would return to the same areas they left, timing their arrival with the melting snows and thawing potholes. As I lay, I wondered how anyone hearing those geese could deny the existence of God.

We understand only a little of their migration, and what we don't know makes us wonder at God's creative wisdom.

The V-shaped formation, we know, helps them conserve energy. Each goose cuts the wind and creates a little air pocket for the goose behind it. The foremost bird must work the hardest. When that goose tires, it drops behind and another goose takes its turn in front. *We* know that this conserves energy, but who told the geese?

We also know that they fly by day and by night, taking an arrow-straight route from their summer to their winter homes. Sometimes they fly thousands of miles on that straight route. Even if we can't see them at night, we know where they are going. Who shows them the way?

We know, too, that they leave the north country when days become shorter. Winter is on its way and food will be hard to find. They will not starve if they fly south. We know this, but who told the geese?

Should a goose choose to rest within sight of some doubter, that person need only look, and surely he would see evidence of a Creator in the design of the bird!

Large webbed feet give a goose swimming power. If the feet were merely toes without webbing, the bird couldn't paddle in the water as easily as it does.

Eyes set on the side of its head allow the goose

to see in front and on either side without moving. If the eyes were set forward, the bird couldn't see danger approach. If the eyes were set farther back, the bird couldn't see food in front.

A flat beak, fit together to form strainers on either side, allows the goose to eat properly. Water flows out of its beak while food is caught in the strainer. A hard "nail" at the tip of its upper beak enables the goose to cut grasses and grains. If the beak were different, how would a goose eat?

We know that geese feet and eyes and beaks are well designed for their way of life. But we only watch geese; we didn't make them. Who did?

Should geese choose to nest near some doubter, that person need only observe, and surely she would see evidence of a Creator in the life of this bird!

When a female goose lays an egg, she plucks downy feathers from her breast and places them around the egg. About twenty-four hours later she lays another egg and repeats the process. She usually lays about six eggs and surrounds each one with down.

After all her eggs are laid, the female has a bare patch where she plucked off her down. She settles this patch against her eggs, transferring her body heat to the eggs to incubate them. While she incubates her eggs, she often stands up and turns them with her beak. Each egg is constantly kept at a temperature of about 101°F. When she leaves the nest, she covers the eggs with down.

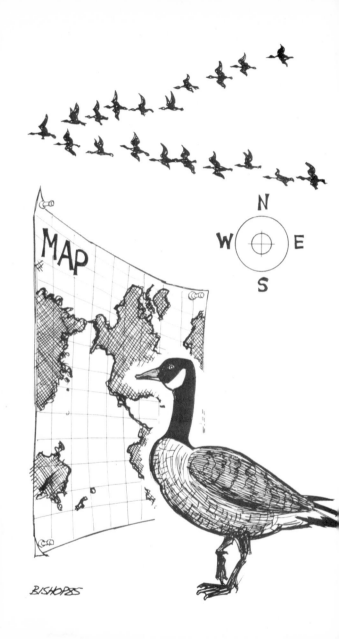

MAP

N
W E
S

BISHOP85

Usually a goose doesn't begin to incubate her eggs until they are all laid. Even if the first and the last eggs were laid six days apart, they will hatch at the same time. The little goslings will grow up together.

When the young goslings hatch they are far from helpless. Within one day they can leave the nest, walk, and swim. Without instruction they know how to swim and dive for cover. This is to their advantage because their nest is usually on the ground, an easy target for badgers, coyotes, skunks, and foxes.

Both the goose (female) and the gander (male) are very protective of their young. As they swim they keep the goslings close to them. One parent always watches for danger and is quick to chase anything that may threaten the family.

Parent geese even molt in a way that protects the family. They change feathers only once a year, while the young are growing their flight feathers. Usually the female molts first. She loses so many feathers that she is unable to fly and has lost most of her defense. But the male still has his old feathers and is able to defend the family. After the female grows her new feathers, the male molts. While he is flightless the female defends the family. Both parents have molted by the time the goslings grow their flight feathers. Now the family can fly together.

Usually flight feathers appear in late summer. Days are becoming shorter, soon it will grow cold. The family is ready. The parents have molted and the young can fly. Soon they will find other geese families and begin their southward journey.

I heard them last night as they flew overhead. I thought about the way a female incubates her eggs and how the new goslings can immediately walk and swim. I wondered at the manner in which the adults molt so that the family can fly when the time is right. I listened as they flew south and I knew that, surely, they would return north in the spring. And I wondered, who can deny that God exists?

13

Dark, Silent Places

Near to all of us there exists a vast, unexplored territory. Not one human being has ever lived there; yet it is populated with millions of beautiful tiny creatures, large ugly creatures, and mammals almost ninety feet long. Huge plants grow there, sometimes as fast as two feet a day, and reach a height of two hundred feet, about as tall as a twenty-story building. This territory has a long chain of mountains that would reach from one coast of North America to the other, rivers so large that our Mississippi would seem like a small creek in comparison, and trenches many miles wider and deeper than the Grand Canyon. A large part of this territory lives in utter, silent blackness and constant near-freezing temperatures. This territory is the strange, wonderful world of our oceans.

We usually think of oceans as big bodies of water that we must cross to go from one continent to another. Not many people stop to think that the oceans are worlds in themselves, covering over twice as much area as all of our continents put together. Not many people stop to think that we couldn't live without our oceans.

People can live for only a short time without water, yet few of us realize that most of our water comes from the oceans. The sun slowly evaporates water from these huge "storage tanks," and it is dropped on the land as rain. All of our lakes and rivers eventually empty into an ocean. The oceans are the biggest part of our life-giving water cycle. Without them the earth would soon dry up.

People like to boast about inventions they have made, like the air conditioner. But man didn't make the first air conditioner; God made the oceans as global air conditioners.

The water in our oceans never stays in the same place; it moves around the earth very slowly. In hot tropical regions the ocean water picks up heat and stores it until it flows toward colder climates. There it releases the heat to the air, warming the surrounding countries. The cooled water then gradually flows toward the warmer climates to help cool the tropical regions of the world.

There are certain parts of the oceans—rivers within oceans—that flow faster than surrounding waters and carry water far north before it has a chance to cool.

The Gulf Stream, which helps to warm Florida, flows faster than a person can walk. This ocean river is over one hundred and fifty miles wide in places and sends off branches that warm the coasts of Norway and Sweden.

Another current, called the Kuroshio Current, helps to heat our western coast and to keep our state of Alaska livable.

Without our oceans and their currents, many parts of our world would be too cold or too hot to live in.

Although we couldn't live without the oceans, people have learned to fear them, and for good reasons. These life-giving waters can also bring death and destruction.

A storm at sea can produce waves as big as an eighty-story building. Some of our largest ships are tossed around like helpless toys in these storms.

Occasionally there are earthquakes on the floor of an ocean. These quakes can produce tidal waves, huge walls of water that come rushing onto land faster than our fastest train. A tidal wave that hit Japan once killed 27,122 people.

Residents of our eastern coast are all too familiar with the death and destruction that comes when a hurricane, born at sea, rushes inland. People certainly have not learned to control the seas yet.

We're all familiar with the sea life that grows

near our shorelines. Many of us have eaten lobster, crab, shrimp, or oysters. We've all seen whales at an aquarium, or watched trained seals or porpoises perform. We use sponges that grow in the ocean, and we make jewelry out of the beautiful coral. Most of the sea life that we know occupies only the shallow fringes of the oceans.

Deep inside their waters our oceans still hold many secrets. There are places where the water is six and one-half miles deep. People can only guess at what lies at the bottom. Sunlight can creep down to about 1,000 feet. Below that there is absolute blackness, six miles of total darkness straight down. The near-freezing water at that depth has such great pressure that a person would be instantly crushed if he or she tried to swim into that mysterious world.

The few fish that scientists have brought up from these dark waters have been especially created to live there. Somehow they can live in greater pressure than people can. Most of them carry their own lights as part of their bodies. No vegetable life can grow in darkness, so the fish must eat each other. Most of them have very large mouths and fierce-looking teeth.

There are many creatures living in these black waters that people have never seen. In experiments with sound waves in the oceans, scientists have discovered that a big, unknown "something" lives over one-half mile beneath the surface of the water. No one knows what that "something" is.

Scientists think that part of the ocean floor is a black, mucky ooze. Anything landing on this ooze gradually sinks down farther than our tallest skyscraper and is never seen again.

It's a little frightening to think of black, mucky ooze; large, unknown creatures; dark, silent places; and uncontrollable storms. Maybe that's why people don't think much about oceans.

We all acknowledge the fact that God gave us oceans to provide us with water and some good things to eat, and to control our weather; but sometimes I think he had a lot more in mind when he created these deep, mysterious waters. After all, when we do think about them we can hardly say that people have mastered the earth. The oceans still remind us that only our Creator knows and controls the whole earth.

14

Beyond the Shells

If you live near an ocean, you may find yourself collecting shells sometime during the summer. Even if you live far inland, some of those shells may find their way into your hands. Or you may find an empty snail shell or a clam from fresh water.

In any case, you'll probably look at the shells and comment on how pretty they are. Then you'll lay them down or try to figure out what to do with them. This summer, try something different with those shells. Don't only look *at* them. Try, in your imagination, to look *beyond* the shells to the creatures that made them.

Those shells weren't always empty, you know. Each one housed a small creature. Each little creature had a role to fill, a special place in creation. Each had a special little body created just right for what it had to do.

Everyone knows what a snail shell looks like. It's rather roundish with spiral curves on each side. Usually it's brown, gray, or mottled brownish-gray. Did you ever think about the creature that lived in that snail shell? It was more than just a slimy body.

All snails have heads with eyes, so they can see where they're going. They also have tentacles—short, thickened "feelers"—to help them find their way. Every snail has a mouth and a sharp, raspy tongue to help it eat. Every snail also has a single flat foot, so it can glide after food.

Some snails eat vegetables—plants that grow in the ocean or near water. Other snails eat meat—clams or other sea creatures. In either case, a snail must be able to find its food, move toward it, and eat it. That's why God gave it eyes, tentacles, a foot, and a mouth with a sharp tongue.

As special protection, each snail also has a tough part of its body called an operculum. That's the snail's door. If the snail feels threatened, it pulls into its shell and covers the opening with this operculum. Hardly anything can reach past this door to the snail's soft body.

A moon snail is a special type of snail that lives in sand near the low-tide mark of our seashores. Its shell is large, smooth, and almost the same shape as an apple. This shell is usually silvery-white, pinkish-tan, or grayish-brown. The moon snail has a very large body, so the opening in the shell is very large. Sometimes the snail's body can stretch three times longer than its shell. In fact, because its body is so large, the moon snail can't stay in its shell very long. It becomes crowded and cramped.

God gave the moon snail something special for its large body. He placed holes around the edges of the moon snail's foot. When the moon snail must curl up into its shell, it squirts water out of its body through these holes. That helps to make the snail's body just a little bit smaller.

Most people know what clam shells look like. They come as a pair, two hinged together. Often you may find only one of the pair. It's hollowed out, shaped like a lopsided bowl. It's usually quite smooth, although there are fine ridges, and it's tannish or grayish.

Clams are completely different from snails. Clams don't have eyes or tentacles or a tongue. Instead, they have one or two tubes which they poke out of their shells. A clam does have a foot, but it's not created for walking, as a snail's is. Instead, it's paddle-shaped for digging.

Clams are different from snails because they were created for a different purpose. They don't eat the same plants or sea creatures that snails eat. Instead, they eat microscopic bits of plants and animals floating in the water. They burrow into sand or mud and strain water to get their food, using siphon tubes. A clam pulls water into

its body through one siphon, strains any bits of food from the water, then shoots the water out of the other siphon.

A clam has no need to walk to its food. As long as the clam is in water, food will come to it. So, instead of a walking-foot, God gave the clam a paddle-foot, which is just right for digging into mud or sand to anchor the clam in place. That foot is also good protection for the clam. When the clam is in danger, it simply digs itself far down into mud or sand, away from its enemies. Some clams can burrow so quickly that it's almost impossible for a human to dig them out of their hiding places.

Because creatures such as snails like to eat clams, God gave the clam extra protection in that double shell. A clam can pull its foot and siphons inside and clamp its shell so tightly that it takes a special force to open it. If you find a clam shell, look on the inside for two small spots. These mark the places where strong muscles held the shell together. Also, try to count the fine ridges

BISHOP 84

on a clam shell. That will tell you how long the clam lived. Each year a clam adds one ridge to its shell. It begins life as small as a pinhead and grows to the size creature whose shell you found.

If you find a bluish-black shell that is long, thin, and almost pointed on top, you may have a mussel shell. Mussels, like clams, strain microscopic bits of plants and animals from water. They too have siphons instead of mouths and tongues. But mussels live and eat in a place different from clams. Mussels settle on rocks, not in mud or sand.

Because mussels live in a different place, God gave them feet different from those of clams. Mussels have tiny glands in their feet. These glands make strong, sticky threads. Each mussel sends several threads out from its foot and attaches the threads to a rock. The threads harden and almost glue the mussel to the rock. Waves and sea currents can't wash the mussel from its home.

Although a mussel has no need to travel, it can "walk." It sends out threads in a new direction, picks up the old threads, and moves. Because it never needs to move more than a few inches, a mussel can "walk" only three or four inches an hour.

Another shell creature that lives on rocks is called a limpet. A limpet has one shell, not two like clams and mussels. A limpet's shell is cone-shaped, like an upside-down pointed bowl. Some limpet shells are ribbed; others are smooth.

Some have a little hole on top. Ribbed limpet shells are usually white. Smooth limpet shells are often a mixture of greens and grays.

Although limpets live on rocks, as mussels do, they are very different from mussels. Limpets are really a special type of snail. They have the snail's foot, eyes, tentacles, and tongue. Limpets help to clean rocks in the oceans. They eat tiny plants that grow on those rocks. That's why God gave them the snail's walking-foot—to crawl over rocks. That's also why he gave them the eyes, tentacles, and tongue. They must see their food and scrape it off the rocks.

Limpets' shells were created a little differently from most snail shells that we know. A limpet can't curl into its shell, because that shell is like an upside-down bowl. But a limpet has no need to crawl into its shell; it is protected by the rock beneath it. A limpet can pull its shell so tightly against a rock that it almost can't be pried off.

In fact, most limpets have special "homes" on their rocks. A certain spot on a rock will fit a limpet's shell perfectly. Either the shell has grown to fit the rock or the creature has worn the rock away to fit its shell. When the rock is covered with water, a limpet will move about and eat. But before the tide goes out and the water leaves the rock, a limpet returns to its special spot on the rock, clamps itself down, and lies protected until water covers it again.

The hole at the top of some limpets' shells is another protection that God provided. You see, starfish like to eat limpets. A starfish will climb over a limpet and try to pry its shell from the rock. When this happens, the limpet can ooze its slippery body through the hole in its shell and cover the shell with its body. The starfish can't grip the slippery body, so the limpet is safe.

Have you ever seen a scallop shell? Or a periwinkle? Or a whelk? These, too, are different, because each creature was created for a different purpose. We could go on and on about shells and the creatures that build them, but we don't have enough space or time to talk about each creature. Yet I'm sure that if you studied each one, you would see that God created it just right for its life.

Shells are interesting and pretty. Yet far more fascinating are the creatures that lived in them. Sometimes it's good to look beyond the shells.

15

Starfish

Have you ever seen a starfish? Simple but beautiful, isn't it? It has five petal-like arms attached to a small, disc-like body. Each of the arms is covered with bumps and small spines, all arranged into beautiful little patterns. The starfish moves slowly over the ocean floor on those arms, and it eats clams. That's about it for the starfish—simple and beautiful.

But wait a minute! Those beautifully patterned bumps and spines are there for a reason, not just for beauty. And should you look inside a starfish, you would find more beautiful patterns, some for very complicated purposes.

Take the way a starfish walks, for example. It doesn't simply move those arms with little muscles. It has a complicated but beautifully patterned system for walking. It's called a water vascular system, and you must look inside the starfish to see it.

Inside that disc-like body lies a circular tube, like a small pipe bent into a perfect circle. It's called a ring canal. It's connected to one small pipe, called a stone canal, that leads from the ring canal to the outside of the starfish body. That stone canal is capped with a sieve.

Connected to this ring canal are five more pipes called the radial canals. Each radial canal runs down the center of a starfish arm. The water that comes into the ring canal flows into each of these radial canals.

Now the starfish becomes more complicated, yet still beautifully patterned.

Connected to each of these radial canals are several smaller pipes. They branch out evenly from both sides of a radial canal, and they're evenly spaced all the way down each radial canal.

At the end of each pipe is a small, hollow cylinder that looks somewhat like an empty balloon. The sac part of the balloon pokes up into the body and is called an ampulla. The part of the balloon that you would blow into is called a tube foot. It hangs down and is connected to the outside of the starfish, the bottom of its arms.

These tube feet account for some of the bumps you see on a starfish. They make such a perfect pattern because the inside of the starfish is such a perfect pattern. But there's a reason for those

tube bumps.

Remember the sieve in the middle of the body, connected to the stone canal, connected to the ring canal, connected to the radial canals? Well, the starfish sucks water in through the sieve. Because the sieve is so fine, only water enters the canals.

Little hairs in the stone canal waft the water to the ring canal. From there it flows to the radial canals, through the little pipes and into the "balloons." There are valves in the smallest pipes, so the water can't back up through the canals.

If the starfish wants to move one arm, it fills its canals with water. Then it squeezes shut all the ampullae—the balloon-like sacs—in one arm. Since the water can't back up, it is forced down into the little tube feet. This pushes out all the tube feet on one arm. These tiny feet grab on to whatever the starfish is walking over. Then they pull the starfish forward.

When the starfish relaxes, water can flow out. Then it's ready to take another step.

Not as simple as you thought, is it? Actually, it's very complicated, but beautiful.

The outer skin of the starfish is also complicated, but beautiful. If you could look at it under a microscope, you would see an even more intricate pattern than you see when you glance at it. Besides the bumps from the tube feet, you would see other bumps scattered around the skin.

If you look closely at these bumps, you can see

that they're spines. They are there to protect the starfish. Any smaller creature trying to crawl over a starfish finds it tough going. There are too many spines in the way.

Set around each of these spines is a row of tiny pincers that looks like a circle of flowers planted around a small tree. If a creature insists on walking over a starfish, these pincers close and give the tiny intruder a nip, encouraging it to leave.

Scattered between the spines are skin gills, sprouting like blades of grass between trees. These skin gills have very thin walls, which make it possible for the starfish to breathe. Oxygen passes from the water through the skin gills into the starfish. Carbon dioxide passes from the starfish to the water.

Because these skin gills are so sensitive, small pincers are placed between them to protect them. If you could look closely at these pincers, you'd see that the inside edge of each pincer is toothed in a regular pattern. This adds to the pinch of the pincers.

A special bump, or spot, lies at the very tip of each arm of the starfish. This is an eyespot. It's sensitive to food and to chemicals in the water. It's at the tip of each arm so that it can sense food quickly. Then the starfish can reach out and look for the food.

A starfish's equipment for catching and digesting food is also very complicated. And it also is set up in a beautiful pattern.

I think you have the idea by now. A starfish is beautiful, yes. It's even more beautiful than you would guess after a quick glance. Its body shows a perfectly balanced design, inside and out, made by a Master Designer.

A starfish is *not* simple. It's a living creature, and no living creature is simple. Every living creature holds secrets that only its Creator knows.

In a way, starfish remind me of people. Take any individual and you'll always find some beauty both inside and out. In any person you'll always find more to learn about and more to appreciate than meets the eye.

16

Not So Simple

Long ago I learned that sponges are simple animals. I don't mean the kind of square, colored plastic sponges that most of us use now. I mean the brownish, shapeless sponge that Grandma used to use and that some of us still use. It's that spongy mass that you find in a few stores; a real *sponge* sponge, not a fake sponge. It's the kind you see in the picture.

I could accept the "animal" part of the "simple animals." I learned that it lives in oceans. It eats, it grows, it dies. It's an animal. By the time you find it at the store, it's dead. When you use a sponge sponge (not a fake sponge), you're using the remains of an animal. That I could accept.

I had trouble with the "simple" part. Just what

did people mean by "simple"? Was a sponge a not-too-smart animal, as in "It's not very smart; it's simple"? But, I thought, a sponge is smart enough to live. It eats, it grows. It must not be altogether simple that way.

Later I was told that a sponge is simple in the sense that it's not complicated. It doesn't have the complicated digestive, nervous, circulatory, muscular, and other systems that some animals have. It's not necessarily dumb-simple. It's just not-complicated-simple.

Recently I decided to learn more about sponges. Since they're not-complicated-simple, I figured I might be able to understand them. I read several books about them, and now *I* feel dumb-simple.

I discovered that sponges are collections of many cells that stick together. In a way, the individual cells can almost make it on their own. Break a sponge up, and the individual cells live for a while and move around. If they contact each other, they stick together. Given enough time, the broken-up sponge can put itself partially together again. That isn't so simple.

When pulled together, a sponge has three different types of cells. The choanocytes are cells with little hairs on them. They drive water through the sponge and collect small bits of food. Each choanocyte has a sticky rim around it that traps the food.

In a fully grown sponge, the choanocytes are enclosed within a wall of epithelial cells. These cells form an outside skin for the sponge. Often the skin is covered with a hard skeleton-like material or with little prickers that make the sponge less edible to fish.

A third type of cell seems to wander between the choanocyte and the epithelial cells. Naturalists think these cells distribute food and secrete the skeleton-like material for the sponge.

A sponge usually has one big opening on the top of its body. Most animals with one opening take food *in* through that opening. The sponge pumps water *out*.

Water enters through tiny holes all over the sponge's body. After it passes the skin cells, water is pumped by the tiny hairs of the choanocyte cells to the hollow sponge center. As the water passes the choanocyte cells, food is filtered out. The water then is pushed out through the big opening.

Sponges can close their openings. Although they have no muscles, the skin, or epithelial cells, are somehow responsible for this. Naturalists aren't quite sure how it works. All they know is, if a living sponge is pricked at its base, the hole at its top will close. It may take thirty seconds to eight minutes for this to happen. Considering the fact that a sponge has no nerves or muscles, this closing is no simple task.

Sometimes even the little pores on a sponge's body may close somehow when they're touched. No simple task for such a simple animal.

Sponges make new sponges in different ways.

Sometimes it happens by budding: a group of cells will break off and form a new sponge.

Sometimes new sponges are formed when an egg and a sperm cell unite. Somehow these are formed by that wandering third type of cell. The sperm burrows into the egg. The egg develops into a solid mass of cells with the "hairy" choanocyte cells on the outside. The egg then breaks out of the parent sponge and settles down to form a new sponge. Suddenly, the cells rearrange so that the choanocyte cells move to the inside and a "mass" of cells moves to the outside and becomes the skeletal layer.

How this all happens, I don't know. How a sponge "knows" to close its pores, I don't know. How a sponge closes its big opening, I don't know. Do you see why I began to feel dumbsimple?

But then, no one knows everything about a sponge. Although we label it a "simple" animal, it's really not so simple to understand. By calling it a "simple" animal, people mean that it's not as complicated as other animals. We don't mean that it's easy to understand. Nothing in God's creation is so simple that we can fully understand it.

Maybe we should call the sponge a not-as-complicated-as-other-animals animal.

17

My Friend the Lobster

A friend of mine went to the beach last week and came back with quite a sunburn. Another friend said of her that she was "red as a lobster."

As soon as she said that, my mind began to play tricks on me. I "saw" our friend lying on a blanket, slowly sprouting extra legs and two huge claws. Her eyes bugged out of her head and wiggled about on two stalks. Her antennae waved around as she slowly crawled off the blanket and into the water.

In my mind's eye she slowly lost her color, too. Her sunburn faded to a lobster's normal mottled brownish green. A lobster isn't red unless it's been boiled in someone's pot. The only similarity between my human friend and my lobster friend is that they both turn red when they're cooked—one in the sun, the other in a pot.

Mentally, I left my human friend on her blanket and followed my lobster friend to the water where it belonged. By some mental miracle, the lake became an ocean, since that's where lobsters live. I marveled as I looked over this sea creature, so different from the lifeless red "tail" I occasionally order at a restaurant.

Lobsters make a good meal, but I'm sure that God didn't create them only for that purpose. Otherwise he wouldn't have made them the way he did.

Created for an underwater life, a lobster doesn't have lungs like ours. Instead, it has a series of feather-like gills set within two chambers in its body. Paddle-like attachments, called bailers, draw water through the gill chamber and over the gills. When the lobster's blood enters the gills, it draws oxygen from the water. That's how a lobster "breathes" in the water.

A lobster heart pumps slightly bluish blood through channels to carry oxygen and nourishment to all parts of the lobster body.

A two-chamber stomach breaks food down so that it can be absorbed by the blood. The first chamber contains hard teeth that grind the food. Between the two chambers a hair-like sieve strains the food. Any chunk that can't pass through the sieve is spit out. The second chamber contains strong juices that break down the food so it can be absorbed by the blood.

Outside as well as in, a lobster has what it needs for its way of life. For example, two pair of long antennae sense vibrations and chemical changes within its watery home. They help tell the lobster what is near, what to avoid, and what to eat.

Its eyes are on movable stalks, so the lobster can see in many directions. It can pull its eyes in when danger threatens.

Five pairs of legs help the lobster crawl across the ocean bottom. The first pair, of course, carries its huge claws.

When a lobster is young, its claws are small for its body. As its body grows, the claws grow faster until they become big, useful tools.

The lobster's two claws are not alike. One is usually heavy and has blunt teeth to crush its prey. The other is smaller and has sharp teeth to cut and tear food. All lobsters don't have the big claw on the same side. Some are "right-handed" and others are "lefties."

What we call the lobster's tail is really its abdomen. Swimmerets, little "feet," are attached to the underside of the abdomen. Female lobsters hold their eggs in the swimmerets.

The lobster's tail is really the two flat "paddles" at the end of its abdomen. These unfold like a fan and enable the lobster to swim backward. If a lobster is disturbed, it will flip its tail to stir up mud or sand as a smoke screen.

Because a lobster lives on the bottom of the ocean and is active mostly at night, its world is

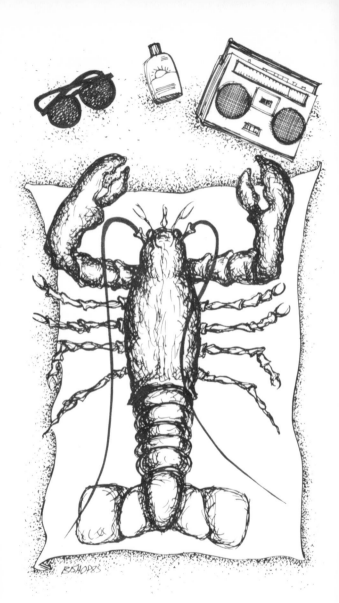

dark and murky. To aid the lobster in "seeing," tiny sensory hairs, called setae, grow all over its body. These short bristles contain nerves by which the lobster can see, smell, and hear.

A lobster's best defense is its hard shell. As the lobster grows, it sheds this shell, or molts. Before molting begins, some lime in the shell dissolves and a new soft shell grows beneath it. The muscles and internal organs shrink slightly. Then the old shell splits down the back and the lobster crawls out of the opening. While the new shell is still soft, the lobster absorbs a lot of water and grows rapidly. It instinctively hides during this time because its soft shell isn't good protection. It also instinctively eats its old shell to obtain the lime that will harden the new shell.

Sometimes a leg or a claw breaks off when the lobster pulls out of its shell. It's hard to pull a big claw through a little joint. But the lobster was created to be able to part with a leg or a claw at a joint without a problem. Its blood clots quickly, so it doesn't bleed to death. In a few days a new leg or claw begins to grow to replace the old one.

A lobster can even part with a leg or claw on purpose if it wants to. If an enemy grabs a claw, the lobster simply flexes some muscles, twists that leg, and leaves the enemy holding only the claw. Of course, it doesn't think about this; it reacts by instinct. But the trick works.

Speaking of thinking, I'd been thinking about lobsters all that time and forgetting the friend I was talking to.

I jerked myself back to reality and tried to listen to what she was saying. I could only think of our sunburned friend. I wondered if she had also become "crabby." But then, maybe she was "happy as a clam" to be "red as a lobster."

18

How Does Hermit Crab Survive?

Hermit Crab is a very delicate fellow. At certain times in his life, a blowing grain of sand could kill him. When he's on shore, a simple blade of grass could cut him in half.

Hermit Crab is also a very delicious fellow. Certain fish and other sea creatures would love to make a meal of Hermit. The sea where Hermit lives swarms with his enemies.

Hermit and his relatives have always lived in the sea. They've been delicate at certain times, and they've always been delicious. Yet there are always lots of hermit crabs in the ocean. If he's so delicate and delicious and lives among so many crabmeat lovers, how does Hermit Crab survive?

Some people say that Hermit Crab is smart.

He does act smart at times. For example, if Hermit Crab has a shell that is too brightly colored, he will cover it somehow. Then it isn't noticed so easily by his enemies. That's smart.

Hermit Crab will often cover his shell with sea anemones. Sea anemones are strange little tube-shaped animals with flowerlike tentacles. With strong grips they stick themselves to rocks beneath the water surface. Most anemones stay in one spot throughout their lives. People usually can't pry living anemones from rocks.

But Hermit Crab can. He runs one claw up and down, up and down an anemone's body. He does this for hours. Finally the anemone foot lets go of its rock. Hermit Crab quickly plants the anemone on top of his shell. Then he rubs the strange tubular body again until the foot takes firm hold of the shell.

Hermit Crab surely does act smart when he covers his shell with anemones. You'd almost guess that he is thinking about protecting himself when he does that. But I suspect that Hermit Crab doesn't really think.

Some people say that Hermit Crab has very good instincts, especially when he changes shells. Since he doesn't grow a shell of his own, he must find an empty shell of some sea creature and crawl inside. But as he grows he must move to bigger shells.

When he feels that he's going to molt, or crawl out of his old skin, instinct seems to tell him that he'll need a bigger shell. So he finds one and hangs on to it with one claw poking out of his present shell. As molting time draws nearer he grips his new shell more tightly. He pulls it closer to his present shell so that no other hermit crab can steal it from him. He seems to sense that he doesn't have long to look for another new shell.

The most dangerous period of Hermit Crab's life is when he moves into his new shell. That's when he's so delicate that a blowing grain of sand could kill him. By instinct he changes shells very quickly. He unhooks a muscle at the end of his body and releases his grip on the old, smaller shell. Slowly he crawls out. Immediately he sticks his tail into the new, bigger shell. He backs in carefully. When he reaches the end of the shell, he grips it with muscles so strong hardly anyone could pull him out. Then he contracts all his muscles and pulls himself deep within the shell.

After he's in the new shell, Hermit Crab can molt. He has room to wiggle and break free from his old skin. Again, working on instinct, he leans far out of his shell so that his old skin can float away.

Hermit Crab surely is OK to have such good instincts. But I suspect that there's something more than luck behind those instincts.

How does Hermit Crab survive? Sometimes it almost seems like he's thinking, but Hermit Crab doesn't really think. Sometimes it seems like he has lucky instincts, but instincts are not a matter of luck.

I know how Hermit Crab survives. Someone created those instincts within the crab's body so that he would do the right things at the right times. Someone took care of Hermit Crab by giving him the right instincts.

Someone? Of course! The same One who cares for you and me.

19

The Incredible Salmon

It was a blind date, and we were going to watch the salmon jump. I chuckled about it for a week before we went. Who goes to watch fish jump? I stopped laughing the night we went.

We drove fifty miles to a little town called Newaygo, on the Muskegon River. "What kind of person will drive fifty miles just to watch fish?" I thought, but I said nothing. We stopped in a little dirt parking lot near the river and scrambled over rocks, through underbrush, and down a bank until we were standing by the river. Just a few yards upstream was a small dam with water flowing over it. Scores of people stood on the riverbank staring at the dam.

"Just watch," he said. So I did.

Suddenly a huge silver-gray fish leaped out of the water toward the dam. Then another jumped, and another. They all lashed their tails violently in an effort to jump as high as they could. Some of them jumped several feet out of the water, almost to the top of the dam. Some hit the dam and fell back into the water, others made it over the dam. Each fish that fell back would swim around a little, face the dam, work up some speed, and jump again. It wouldn't give up.

It was incredible. Those salmon were trying to jump over the dam, and nothing was going to stop them. Some strong instinct urged them to jump again and again until they either made it over the dam or were too tired to try.

These salmon had at one time lived upstream, he told me. Then at one point in their lives they had swum down all the way to Lake Michigan. Now they were coming back to spawn (lay their eggs). Instinct sent them to the same spot in the river from which they had started. If a dam were in the way, they would try with all their might to jump it.

These salmon were not natural to the Muskegon River, he went on to inform me. They had been planted—hatched in a fish hatchery and put into the river when they were young. Salmon live naturally only in rivers that empty into the Pacific or Atlantic Oceans. Their life stories are incredible. We'll probably never understand the instincts created within these fish.

A female salmon looks for a bed of gravel on

the bottom of the river. That's where she'll lay her eggs. She scoops away some of the gravel with her tail to make a hollow pocket, then lays her eggs in the pocket. After a male salmon fertilizes the eggs, she scrapes gravel over them. Then they're protected.

A female salmon lays thousands of eggs. If she weighs twenty pounds, she may lay from 14,000 to 16,000 eggs. If she's bigger, she may lay still more. She was created to lay this many because salmon eggs, little salmon, and even big salmon have many enemies. If a few salmon are to live, she must lay many, many eggs.

And, by instinct, she lays her eggs in just the right place. Gravel helps purify water, so the water that filters over the eggs is fresh and clean. Should a violent flood occur, large boulders washed downriver would tumble right *over* the hollow in which the eggs lay. Mud and silt don't choke the eggs because they're covered with a protective layer of gravel. Yet some of the eggs usually are damaged. Only about half of them will hatch.

If the water is cold, the eggs develop very slowly. As the water warms, development quickens. The fish never hatch in winter, only in spring as the water is warming.

At first the little salmon (called alevins at this stage) stay right in the gravel bed, under gravel. Danger may lurk above, and they're not strong enough to deal with it. Though they don't realize this, instinct keeps them below the gravel. Each alevin has a little yolk sac attached to its body. It uses this as food for a few weeks.

When the yolk sac is digested, the alevin is strong enough to break through the gravel and fend for itself. It's only about an inch long, but it can sense what is danger and what is food.

At first the little fish eats only microscopic river plants and animals. But as it grows, it eats insects and worms. However, it must also be alert for large insects, larger fish, and birds and animals that would like to eat it.

A little salmon may stay in a river for one to three years, depending on what kind of salmon it is. During this time it grows several inches and goes through stages in which it's called a fry, a fingerling, and then a parr.

Then something suddenly happens to it. It's seized with an urge to swim downriver.

Lots of fish are content to spend their whole lives in one river or one part of a river, but not the salmon. No one can explain the urge, but it's there. The salmon suddenly begins to swim downriver toward the ocean. Then it's called a smolt.

Some smolts may have to travel only a few miles to reach ocean water. Some travel hundreds of miles. Instinct urges them on as far as they must go until they reach the ocean.

When they reach the ocean, salmon really begin to grow. Some kinds are big at seven pounds, but others may grow to twenty-five pounds or more.

We don't know exactly what salmon eat or where they go in the oceans. We only know that they grow a lot, and some of them travel many, many miles from their home river.

Some kinds of salmon stay in the ocean for a year. Some kinds may stay for five years. But sometime in its life every salmon feels the instinct to return to its home river.

Then the incredible journey begins. From somewhere out in that enormous ocean, each salmon sets a course to its home stream. Some fish may travel thousands of miles, guided by instinct, to find their way home.

Scientists don't know how salmon can find their way to exactly the right river. Some say they follow sea currents or smell their way. Others say they're guided by magnetic forces in the earth. No one really knows. Salmon were created with an instinct that we can't understand. But that instinct guides them directly to the places where they hatched.

Along the way the salmon once more undergo changes. Their stomachs shrink and they lose their interest in food. Some males develop hooked jaws, and all males produce milt to fertilize eggs. Females produce thousands of eggs. They are interested only in going "home" and spawning.

At this point, almost nothing will stand in their way, so strong is their instinct. They'll swim thousands of miles, push upstream for weeks or months and struggle mightily to avoid bears and nets that scoop them out of the water. They'll run rapids, jump twelve-foot waterfalls, and butt tirelessly against dams. They'll struggle upstream, sometimes covering twenty-five miles in a day. Hundreds of salmon that hatched in the same river will struggle together night and day to reach home. A few will make it.

Those that do are usually tired, battered, and bruised. But they find their gravel beds and spawn. Some salmon—those that live in the Atlantic—may recover, go to sea, and return to spawn again. Most salmon die after they spawn once, however.

But their lives have been completed. Guided by instincts that we'll probably never understand, they have traveled incredible distances and fought against unbelievable odds.

Some of them even managed to jump that dam in the Muskegon River. Of course they were only planted upriver, not born there, but they followed the same instincts. And some of them made it "home." I watched them go. Amazing!

What about that blind date that took me to watch the salmon jump? He turned out to be a pretty good guy. In fact, I married him.

Our cabin in the woods is on a lonely stretch of the Muskegon River. Every autumn now we walk along the riverbank and watch the salmon spawn.

20

Recipe for a Jellyfish

2 clear plastic bags
1 bag tie
water
food coloring (if desired)
pinch of salt

Fill one bag about half-full of water. Add a pinch of salt.
Add a few drops of food coloring if you wish.
Carefully push the second bag inside the first.
Add a little water to the second bag.
Tie the mouths of the two bags together with the bag tie.
Tuck in the corners.
Turn the bags over and float in water.
Presto! You have a jellyfish!

The outer plastic bag is the jellyfish skin. The water in that bag is the jelly under the skin. (Some jellyfish have colored jelly, some have clear. Sometimes a jellyfish changes its color.) The inner plastic bag is the jellyfish stomach. The place where you've tied the bags together is the mouth. The edges of the bags are jellyfish arms, or tentacles. You've made a jellyfish!

There's one problem with this recipe, though. You have something that only *looks* like a jellyfish. It won't *act* like one. You see, the recipe isn't quite complete. We're missing some ingredients.

When God makes a jellyfish, he makes the jelly part out of about ninety-six percent water, three percent salt, and one percent proteins and carbohydrates. This last one percent is the part that makes the jelly firm.

We can't figure out that part of the recipe. Such a small amount of protein and carbohydrates shouldn't make such a large amount of salt water firm. That's like taking two cups of fruit juice and trying to turn it into jelly with one teaspoon of gelatin. Any cook knows that a recipe like that won't work. But somehow God makes it work for a jellyfish.

Our recipe has another slight problem. We can't make plastic bags grow. A jellyfish's body swells with water, which becomes jelly as protein from its food is added. When the jellyfish doesn't eat much, its body shrinks. Even the outer skin shrinks, but it doesn't wrinkle like our plastic bag would. Whether a jellyfish is shrinking or growing, inside its body the water, salt, protein, and carbohydrates always remain in the right balance.

If you'd look closely at a real jellyfish, you'd see a few things our plastic bag model doesn't have. For example, a ring of muscle cells usually circles the bottom of the jellyfish. These muscle cells are part of the skin and are somehow connected to the jelly. When the muscles contract, or pull together, the "outer plastic bag" pulls together. Water squirts out of the stomach and drives the jellyfish forward. The muscles relax, the "bag" opens, and water pours into the stomach. The muscles contract again, the "bag" pulls together, and the jellyfish moves again.

A jellyfish doesn't have a heart or blood like we do. It doesn't need such things to live. As it moves, seawater is constantly pumping in and out of its body. The water brings oxygen to all parts of the jellyfish body. So seawater takes the place of jellyfish blood.

A jellyfish also has no brain, but it does have a ring of nerves. This ring lies along the muscle ring and makes the muscle beat more slowly or more quickly.

Another smaller nerve ring controls the mouth. It stops the muscle ring that makes the jellyfish move and starts some muscles that open the mouth. Most jellyfish can't swim and eat at the same time.

Now look at the loose edges of your plastic

bags. They are the jellyfish arms, or tentacles. Some jellyfish have short tentacles, crowded closely together. They look a lot like the ruffled edges of a plastic bag. Other jellyfish have long, snakelike tentacles.

A jellyfish has no tongue or nose, so it can't taste or smell as we do. But it does have skin cells that can sense the presence of living creatures in the water. These skin cells are usually located on its tentacles and around its mouth. As the tentacles move up, down, and around in the water, the jellyfish is "tasting" and "smelling" all around itself.

The "tentacles" on your plastic bags are harmless. A plastic bag doesn't sting—but a real jellyfish does. We couldn't possibly make a recipe for jellyfish stingers. They're too complicated.

You can't see a stinger without a microscope.

The most you may notice is ridges or lumps made by clusters of stingers. Each stinger is a tiny capsule of poison with a long, hollow thread coiled inside it. The capsule and thread are buried beneath the skin. One tiny trigger hair juts out from the skin above where the stinger is buried.

If a fish brushes the trigger hair, the stinger immediately uncoils and shoots out from the skin. The tiny hollow thread cuts into the fish, and poison from the capsule flows into the fish. Sometimes a small fish can trigger fifty or more stingers with a few simple movements. A big fish may trigger 100,000 or more shots.

A jellyfish isn't a big, mean creature just looking for things to sting. In fact, it has no control over its stingers. If the trigger hairs are touched, the stingers are fired, even if the jellyfish isn't hungry. Humans can trigger jellyfish stingers, but jellyfish don't eat people. (Many jellyfish stings are too small for people to notice. Some, however, can make a person very sick.)

Not absolutely everything triggers these stingers. Brush a jellyfish tentacle with an oar or a piece of wood, and very few stingers fire. We can't figure that out, but it works well for a jellyfish.

Not all stingers sting, either. Some shoot out threads that lasso the prey. Others shoot out strings of slime that hamper the prey's movement.

Each stinger is used only once. After it has uncoiled and shot, it can't be put back. That doesn't seem to bother the jellyfish because its body keeps making more. We don't know how or where in its body the jellyfish makes stingers. That's another part of the recipe we can't figure out.

Even if we did figure out how to make stingers, we wouldn't have a complete recipe. We'd have to make some muscles and put some nerves in place. That might be rather difficult. The hardest part, I think, would be figuring out that one percent protein-carbohydrate ingredient. That seems to be what gives the jellyfish life.

I guess we'll have to settle for the plastic-bag-and-water recipe. At least we can see approximately what a jellyfish looks like. I don't think we'll ever figure out the real recipe completely. We don't know how to make the most important ingredient—life. Only God can do that.

21

Florence: A Fable about a Flounder

Florence figured that she was not an ordinary fish. She *knew* that she was a very unusual flounder. From the moment she hatched in her watery home, she sensed that she was different—better, she thought, than other flounders.

The first thing she had seen was a grownup flounder resting on the sea bottom. He had hardly moved as she floated above him. He'd only dug himself deeper into the sand and watched. "That silly old fool," Florence thought. "Doesn't he know that fish are supposed to swim? How lazy he is! I'll never spend my time lying on the ocean bottom." And she swam away.

Within one day Florence had convinced herself that she was indeed unusual. After all, she swam well and gracefully. The adult flounders she had seen swimming didn't seem to know what they were doing. They swam on their sides. "Like floating doormats," Florence sneered as she checked to make sure her back was up and her belly down. "They don't even know how to swim. That's probably why they lie on the bottom so often." And she darted quickly after a tiny fish.

"I'm glad I don't act like them or look like them," she thought with a shudder of disgust. "Why, their mouths are lopsided and some of them have teeth on only one side. Their heads are crooked and their eyes aren't even in the right place. Who ever heard of a fish with both eyes on one side of a crooked head? They're so ugly, no wonder they want to hide."

And hide they did. If they rested in sand, they became yellowish-brown. When they moved to a darker bottom, they became darker. Over pebbles they became blotched, and over bigger stones they became spotted. Florence had trouble finding some adults because they hid so well. "Who wants to associate with those ugly, lazy old flounders anyway?" she thought as she swam serenely above them. "I'm too unusual to be seen with them."

Once more she flitted past an old discarded piece of sheet metal and checked her reflection. "Now, there's a good-looking flounder," she thought. "My eyes are where they belong, one on each side of my head. My coloring is a perfect silver-grey. No need to change that. And my shape is pretty good, too—a regular streamlined fish shape."

Had Florence noticed any other young flounder, she might have seen that it looked exactly like her. Every one of her kind, at her age, has an eye on each side of its head, a silver-grey color, and a streamlined fish shape. But Florence didn't notice other young flounders. She was too busy admiring herself and sneering at the adults.

She was also too busy eating food and dodging enemies. In fact, every day that Florence lived she had to eat more food and dodge more enemies. She liked to eat fish smaller than she. These she could catch quite easily as she swam smartly near the water surface. But as she ate, she grew. The larger she grew, the more tempting she became as dinner for a larger fish. So she had to watch continuously for food and for enemies. "At least I can see what's coming on both sides with my properly placed eyes," she comforted herself.

One day, Florence cruised low in the water to sneer at an adult flounder. She happened to notice that it was eating a small sea urchin, so she tried one herself. Very tasty. She swooped down to the bottom to pick up a sand dollar. That was delicious. Swimming near the bottom, she saw another adult munch on a crab. Still another, she noticed, ate a lobster. So she tried those, too. They were almost tastier than fish.

By the time she was four days old, Florence had developed a definite taste for those little creatures that scuttle along the sea bottom. She found herself spending more time deep in the water looking for those tidbits. But now Florence had a problem. Twice she had almost been eaten when a larger fish had swooped down on her. She hadn't been looking up. She hadn't seen the fish coming.

Actually, Florence had two problems. Not only did she have trouble dodging enemies, but she also had trouble catching food. The crabs and lobsters always saw her coming and scuttled away. To catch the sea urchins and sand dollars, she almost had to stand on her head. Florence was becoming hungry and scared.

By her fourth night, Florence knew she was in trouble. She could hardly catch her favorite foods. She was afraid of big fish and she was tired. Besides that, she had a headache. Bone-tired, she swam over to her sheet metal to check herself. She hoped the strain wasn't showing on her beautiful body.

Wait! What was that? Something was wrong. She knew as soon as she looked. Her eye, her left eye, had moved! Right now, it was moving! And her mouth was crooked! Oh, no. What could she do? Quickly she swam away and hid. Had Florence bothered to ask another flounder, she would have learned the truth. But she didn't ask; she hid.

The truth is that every flounder changes. One eye actually does move from one side of its head to the other side. Its body becomes flat. The lower, blind side fades to almost white, and the upper side develops the marvelous ability to change color. Its mouth becomes twisted and develops teeth on the lower side. Inside, it loses an air sac that helped it swim. In a complicated shift of muscles and nerves, the whole fish changes.

While Florence changed, she hid. At first she was shocked, then she was disappointed. Soon she would become an ugly adult flounder, she thought.

A week after Florence went into hiding, she could stand it no longer. She was too weak and hungry. Slowly she slipped from her hiding place and slid to the ocean floor. Within five minutes she had found her favorite food. Gratefully she gobbled a sand dollar and snatched a sea urchin. A crab ambled past her, and she grabbed it. A lobster soon followed, and she ate that, too.

Only when she had finished the lobster did Florence begin to appreciate her changes. Her skin had changed to match the sea bottom. She was flat, so she didn't make a telltale lump in the sand. Both the crab and the lobster had walked nearby because they hadn't noticed her. She had eaten the sand dollar easily because she had teeth on the lower side of her mouth. And all this time she had stared upward, looking for enemies. Her eyes, those wonderful eyes, could look backward and forward at the same time. As long as Florence stayed on the bottom, she realized, she would be safe from enemies. And she would have plenty of food.

Florence lay on the bottom for a very long time thinking about her body and the way it had changed. She didn't know Who had made those changes or how, but she was beginning to understand why. Slowly she munched her food as she watched a large fish swim overhead, unaware of her presence.

As she lay thinking, she noticed a very young flounder dart through the water above her. He looked just as she had several days earlier. As he darted away, she heard him say, "That silly old fool. How lazy and ugly she looks." Florence remained silent, but smiled a lopsided grin. She had learned. Never again would she call an older flounder a silly old fool. Instead, she would talk with it. Perhaps it would know something she had not yet learned.

And, never, never again would she sneer at a fish different from her. After all, there probably is a very good reason for the difference.

22

Mermaids and Manatees

Believe it or not, a certain sea creature was once mistaken for a mermaid. Or so the story goes.

Let me tell you right off what mermaids are, in case you don't know. First, there are no such things as mermaids. They live only in people's imaginations. They're supposed to be creatures that are half-woman, half-fish. The woman part is always supposed to be very beautiful. Nobody says much about the fish part, but the imaginary mermaid always lives in water.

Now you're probably wondering what that sea creature is. It's a manatee, a type of sea cow. It's real. It lives in warm water, but it breathes air.

The story goes that, long ago, sailors on a

warm part of an ocean spotted some manatees coming up for air. A female manatee was holding her baby with one flipper as she surfaced. The sailors must not have been able to see very well, or the manatees must have been quite far away. Anyway, the sailors thought they had seen a half-woman, half-fish creature. Thus the legend of mermaids was born.

Some people say that the story doesn't make any sense. After all, they argue, just look at manatees. They're ugly.

I suppose that, by people standards, manatees are less than beautiful. They're about ten feet long, weigh more than a ton each, and are shaped like blimps. Their tough skins are about one inch thick and colored a dull brownish-gray. They have paddle-like front flippers and flat tails. Their snouts look like turned-down hippo snouts covered with thick bristles. Their upper lips are divided into two lobes and their chins—if you can call them chins—seem to wrinkle into nothing behind their mouths. They have tiny eyes and smaller earholes.

But that's people standards. By manatee standards, I suppose manatees are well-built. Their bulk and thick hide keep them well-protected in cooler waters. Their flippers help them move along the bottoms of rivers, and their tails help them swim in deeper water. Their turned-down snouts are aimed right at the plants they like to eat, and those bristles help grasp food. Their eyes, although small, function equally well in light or dark water. Those eyes also are lined with oil glands to protect them from the harsh effects of salt water. Their ears are sensitive enough to hear another manatee 150 feet away.

Yet no person has ever called manatees beautiful.

The manatees' real beauty lies in their character. They are some of the most gentle creatures on earth. They eat only water plants. They will not chase, catch, bite, or even bother any living animal or sea creature.

Manatees will not fight other living animals, even to defend themselves. They would rather swim away. A mother manatee will only "screech" if her baby is bothered; she will not attack. If a person swims gently in manatee waters, the creatures will browse undisturbed. Sometimes one will even nuzzle a swimmer or allow that swimmer to pet it.

Manatees prefer to live alone and will simply leave if their home becomes too crowded or noisy. They do seem to enjoy each other's company once in a while. While together, manatees will "tickle" each other with their flippers, "hug" each other, swim and eat together. They "talk" to each other with squeals, chirps, and squeaks.

Manatees' lives are dictated by the weather. Because they can't survive in cold water, they must live around warm springs and rivers in the winter. During the summer they can disappear into warm, shallow ocean waters.

There's one thing that bothers me about the

mermaid-manatee story. If you tell people that manatees were once mistaken for mermaids, they usually ask, "What's a manatee?" They don't ask, "What's a mermaid?" Even though mermaids are make-believe and manatees are real, people know more about mermaids than they do about manatees.

For many years people didn't bother to find out much about manatees, probably because the creatures neither helped nor harmed humans. They were just there, lumpy animals browsing on sea plants in warm springs and warm coastal waters.

In our part of the world, manatees live around the coasts of Florida and Georgia. They used to swim undisturbed in coastal waters. During cold weather they would come into the mouths of rivers and browse around warm springs unseen. Not many people lived there at that time, so not many people saw manatees.

Recently, however, people have become more interested in manatees. More people have moved south and have seen the creatures. Manatees' home waters have been turned into tourist attractions and into waterways for motorboats. Floodgates have been built and canals dug where manatees used to swim. Props from motor boats sometimes hit manatees and kill them. Open floodgates suck manatees under water for longer than they can hold their breath, and the manatees drown. People even pester the manatees because the gentle, slow creatures get in their way.

Now people wonder about this creature: How does it live? Why is it here? How can we stop killing it? Some even wonder *why* or *if* we should stop killing it.

There aren't many manatees left now. They're being killed faster than they can reproduce. At the rate their numbers are dwindling, they'll soon have one thing in common with mermaids—they'll live only in people's imaginations.

Right now mermaids and manatees are very different. People imagined mermaids. Mermaids never really lived. But God created manatees. They do live. Maybe, if we're careful, mermaids and manatees will always be very different.

23

Walrus: A-OK

Walruses are like some people. Or maybe I should say some people are like walruses, since walruses were created first.

I have vague memories of a great big man that looked like a walrus. I can't remember his name or even where I saw him. I just remember looking at his short, thick neck, his tiny eyes, and his whiskery mustache and thinking, "That poor guy looks just like a walrus." I didn't think he was very good-looking.

Most people don't think walruses are very good-looking either. A walrus's wrinkled skin, beady little eyes, bristly mustache, and huge tusks certainly wouldn't win any beauty contest. In fact, they sort of turn people off. Besides that, walruses are so big—they can be almost twelve feet long and weigh nearly a ton—that some people are scared of them. Most people don't even bother to think about that big ugly animal.

Of course, "ugly" is only from our point of view. A walrus is probably perfectly happy to look like a walrus.

Those big tusks—really overgrown teeth—are his digging tools. Walruses usually eat clams and mussels, which they dig from the ocean floor or scrape off rocks with their tusks. If they wear their tusks down a bit, no problem. The tusks keep growing throughout the walrus's life. Some grow tusks that are three and one-half feet long and weigh up to twelve pounds. They may be long and heavy for the walrus to carry around, but they certainly are useful.

Baby walruses aren't born with those tusks. After all, tusks are teeth, and they take about two years to grow. Mama Walrus usually nurses her baby for almost two years. Then its tusks are long enough for it to get its own food.

Even that bristly mustache you see on a walrus has a purpose. It actually helps shovel food into his mouth. Usually there's around four hundred separate bristles. They all have lots of blood vessels and nerve cells in them, so they're very sensitive. After a walrus picks up a clam with his tusks, he'll break it apart. Then he'll clean off the extra junk (pieces of shell, etc.) and push the soft part into his mouth. He does the cleaning and the pushing with his mustache.

Walruses are big and fat—especially fat. They may have up to six inches of blubber stored beneath their two-inch-thick hides. That fat isn't there just because they eat too much. It's there to keep them warm. They sleep in snow and ice and swim in near-freezing water. That layer of blubber acts as insulation between a walrus's warm insides and cold outsides.

Walrus eyes are small, but they're sharp in the water. Their ears look like little folds of skin, but they also are sharp. And their nostrils have special muscles to close the holes when a walrus swims underwater.

Walruses also have strange pouches that open into the back of their throats. A walrus can blow up these pouches like balloons, seal them off, and keep them blown up for hours. Some people think that the animal uses these like a life jacket (or life collar), so it can sleep in the water and still breathe air.

But that's all describing what a walrus looks like and why. Have you ever wondered what a walrus *is* like, not what it *looks* like? Probably not, but I'm going to tell you anyway. They're really neat animals.

They like to live together in herds, swimming, sleeping, and searching for food together. They're noisy, both awake and asleep. As they swim and eat, they often bellow and trumpet at each other. People say that you can hear them for miles—noisy things! When they sleep, they breathe deeply and even snort and snore loudly.

Watching a herd of walruses go to sleep can really be quite entertaining. First, they all hoist themselves up on a big chunk of ice. One after another they'll heave and roll themselves out of the water. Then they start pushing, jostling, and shoving for a place to sleep. Finally they just drape all over each other. Soon they're all hissing, wheezing, and snoring, fast asleep. If one should waken to roll over, or jump in his sleep, the whole group generally snorts, fusses, and juggles around. Then they settle down again.

Walruses sleep often and for long periods of time. Sometimes they can sleep for thirty-six hours straight. That's a full day and a half.

Sunbathing is another popular pastime. Again they snort and grind and bump all over each other to get on an ice floe. In fact, sometimes—just when they all get up there—the walruses' weight is too much for the ice. Under or over it goes, and all the animals are back where they started from.

If a herd is out of the water, one walrus is usually awake and keeping watch. If he senses danger, he'll give a low, whistling bellow and the whole herd will pour into the sea.

Walruses can really move pretty fast on land when they're pushed, but they prefer to move in water. Their flippers work better there.

They're not normally aggressive. This means that they'e not big bullies toward other animals or people. They'd really rather run than fight. A female may fight a killer whale which is after her pup, but normally they fall all over each other running away from danger.

They don't fight much between themselves either. Once in a while they'll argue about who's going to sleep where. But even when they look angry, they're usually bluffing. One big "bully" may rear up on his flippers, push out his chest, and raise his head so his tusks point straight out. He may even "pouff pouff" through his lips and pretend to jab with his tusks, but it's all a big bluff. Walruses prefer to live in peace with each other.

As a matter of fact, they often help each other. Older bull (male) walruses will protect younger bulls from danger. Cows (females) that don't have any babies will often cooperate with young bulls to help take care of any orphaned calves. If a walrus is wounded, another walrus will often support it while it's swimming.

People who have studied walruses tell all sorts of stories about how the animals help each other. One naturalist saw a polar bear creep up on a young bull walrus. The bear didn't know that a big bull was watching. Just as the bear made his first lunge for the small walrus, the big one turned on the bear furiously and killed it.

Another naturalist saw three cows drive a she-bear into the sea and gouge her to death with their tusks. The bear had killed a calf, and the three walruses were enraged.

That's what I mean when I say that walruses are neat. When you really get to know them, you find out that they're good to each other. In some sort of animal sense they seem to care for each other and help each other. That, I think, is beautiful.

I guess you have to look beyond the appearance of a walrus. Most people think they're ugly, and they may be right. But most people haven't looked beyond the fat and the mustache to find out what walruses are really like. Beneath it all they're A-OK.

That's what I meant when I said that some people are like walruses. They may not be good-looking; in fact, they may really be quite ugly in other people's opinions. Often, not many people know them because not many people look beneath the skin. But if you take the time to look, you might find that beneath it all these people are A-OK.